They Don't Understand DEPRESSION

Saying What You're
Not Supposed to Say
and Finding
Meaning in the Dark

Copyright © 2025 Michael D. Griffith

All rights reserved.

No portion of this book may be reproduced, distributed, or transmitted in any form without prior written permission from the author or publisher. The views expressed herein are solely those of the author.

Published in Lehi, UT by Acacia Tree Media Inc. Contact the author or publisher at the following websites:

TheyDontUnderstand.com
MichaelDGriffith.com
AcaciaTreeMedia.com

Library of Congress Control Number: 2024923637

ISBN: 978-1-938374-22-7 (paperback)
ISBN: 978-1-938374-21-0 (hardback)
ISBN: 978-1-938374-20-3 (e-book)

Contents

Part I: What They Don't Understand

1. Introduction 5
2. Negativity 11
3. Judgment 17
4. Dissociation 25
5. Overwhelm 31
6. Guilt 39
7. Hopelessness 47
8. Loneliness 57

Part II: Commit to the Rules

9. How NOT to die 63
10. How to Live 73

Part III: Strengthen the Body

11. Medicine 83
12. Healthfulness 91
13. Alternatives 101

Part IV: Govern the Mind

14. Cooperation 107
15. Triggers 119
16. Lies 125

Part V: Yield to the Spirit

17. Meaning 135
18. Sacrifice 145

Part VI: Final Thoughts

19. Responsibility 153
20. How to Help 161

Afterword 179
Appendix: Summary 181
Acknowledgements 183

NOTE: If you feel too depressed and the thought of reading this book seems overwhelming, please download the audiobook version of this text at: TheyDontUnderstand.com

Part I: What They Don't Understand

1
Introduction

I hate Christmas! ... But you're not allowed to say that. If you say it out loud, it sucks all the joy out of the room for everyone else.

I bet there is something others expect you to enjoy, for which your happy face is also a lie—but you're not really allowed to talk about it ... because ... something must be wrong with you!

We're not allowed to actually tell the truth in polite society. I hate Christmas! I live a lie. I go through the motions to make everyone else "happy," or, at least, spare unnecessary offense. I feel forced to participate in others' Christmas gratification against my will. Every fake smile, every social tradition, every classic movie, every upbeat holiday song, and every end-of-the-year party piles more obligations onto my back when I couldn't even handle the weight before. It requires every excruciating scintilla of strength to make it through December without breaking down in public.

Every holiday platitude, greeting, and cliché feels like a patronizing lecture that proves only that I am different. Whatever they feel, I don't feel it. Everything I feel is bottled up and held back from public view as much as physically possible, but the dam begins to crack.

I try to keep to myself so that I don't explode and vomit my emotions all over those around me, but they don't let you stay out of it, do they? They hound you, and belittle you, and physically coerce you to participate.

For you, that suffocating weight might be something other than Christmas. For you, it's probably a lot of something elses. Whatever it is that forces you to hold back a breaking dam, they don't understand!

They can't understand.

I'm not sad. I'm not mad. And I'm not trying to be mean! I'm "depressed"—as if that word actually describes anything.

They think I should feel like they do. It has never occurred to them that I feel something they have not experienced. I feel confused, numb, unsatisfied, guilty, overwhelmed, worthless, anxious, afraid, hopeless, and tired—but mostly, I feel alone. I am surrounded by people who can't understand. I see a color in the world that they cannot see—and it's ugly. I hear a sound that they cannot hear—and it's so very annoying. I smell an odor they cannot sense—and it's disgusting.

Worse, they feel a joy that I cannot quite remember. They feel an optimism that just doesn't make sense. They feel love that I can only imagine—if I could imagine it—but it's getting harder to do that.

They think I can just decide to quit acting out my depression like I can shut off the imaginary world of a video game—but I can't quit. I can never quit playing. I'm not allowed to quit, because it's not actually a game. I'm trapped in an emotional gauntlet, and every attempt to escape results in another obstacle tightening a noose around my neck.

If I tell the truth, I hurt people. If I lie, I hurt people. If I keep playing, I will explode—and hurt people. If I quit ... well, there is only one way to quit ... and when the depression extinguishes the last flicker of my life, I will forever after be blamed for selfishly hurting people.

The family, the doctors, the therapists, the coworkers, the friends, the bloggers, the media, Hollywood, the church, the culture

—they prove with every word that they don't understand! Because they don't understand, there are a lot of things you and I are not allowed to say.

They want me to say that "Christmas is my favorite time of year," or perhaps that "I cherish the memories," or that it holds so much "meaning." At worst, they might accept "It's not my favorite holiday." Maybe, I'm allowed to say *that*, but *that* is a lie! In this book, I will tell *you* the actual, honest, forbidden truth. I hate Christmas!

Below, I have transcribed some of the lyrics to Blaine Larsen's country song, "How Do You Get That Lonely?"

> *How do you get that lonely, how do you hurt that bad?*
> *To make you make the call, that havin' no life at all,*
> *Is better than the life that you had ...*
> *Did no one see the writing on the wall? ...*
> *I know hindsight's 20/20, but I still don't understand.*
> *How do you feel so empty, you want to let it all go?*
> *How do you get that lonely, and nobody know?*

Why does the author sing that "no one sees the writing on the wall?" Why? Because we're not allowed to write on the wall. That's not appropriate behavior. We're not allowed to say it out loud. You're supposed to hide the pain. That's what people expect. Revealing it to people who don't understand just makes it worse.

If you relate more to the author of these lyrics who "doesn't understand" how someone feels utterly alone, than to the subject who chose to shut off the game, then reading this book probably won't help you. When I say out loud the things that we are not allowed to say, it won't make you understand. Merely reading the words I write without understanding the emotions behind them may make you more judgmental, more confused, and less understanding of someone with depression.

If you are my family member or close friend, please don't read this book. Trust me, you don't want to know the truth. Also, if you don't know me, and have not personally been severely depressed to the point that death looked like a step up, then I don't want you to read this book either. Instead, fast forward to the final chapter titled "Chapter 20: How to Help." I wrote only that final chapter for those who don't understand. Everything else in this book will make sense only to those on the inside.

I will say out loud all of those things that "they" don't understand about *me*. This book is purely my own perspective. Nevertheless, even though my words are entirely self-centered, this book is not really about *me*. I will describe exactly how depression weighed me down for most of my adult life, not because I want you to know about me. I don't! I want you to know that, first, others do know how it feels when "they don't understand" and, second, you can find purpose and peace even in the chains of suffering. I will share how I found meaning in my suffering in the hope that something I share will help you find meaning in your own.

But—

First, I want to prove to you that I understand how it can make sense that "havin' no life at all is better than the life that you [have]." I will describe a lot of very depressing thoughts and emotions. I will describe hell and its demonic tyranny in excruciating detail. I don't want to say it out loud, but you need to know that I know what it feels like when "they don't understand."

You're supposed to be strong. Right? *Mind over matter!* You're supposed to control your emotions. You're supposed to put on a strong face. You're supposed to tough it out. You're supposed to pretend. You're supposed to endure. You're supposed to lie! … Right? And they wonder why "no one sees the writing on the wall."

You know what it's like to go in public and see others with real-life, legitimately happy faces. Or are they just pretending? Someone out there must get it, but you will never know, because society says they are not allowed to tell the truth out loud. That means you have to be alone. You are not allowed to see how others really feel, and they are not allowed to see how you really feel. It's a perfect recipe for hell.

I'm not preaching to you, whether you believe in the devil, nor whether or not you participate in any religion. "Hell" is just the best metaphor I've got. I'm willing to share what I don't actually want to expose about myself because I know something about you. Because you have felt the hell of depression yourself, you won't judge me like "they" do. *You* will understand. In fact, I'm confident that not only will you understand, you will actually feel better knowing that you are not alone.

I apologize in advance, because as I describe my hellfire, you will relive some of yours. I cannot promise you salvation from that abyss. I can only share the lessons that helped me cope after 21 years in the pit. I pray that something I share will help you cope with your own personal hell.

Part one will be depressing and hopeless, so, before continuing, please promise yourself that you will continue all the way to the end, until you also hear about how I found meaning in that abyss.

In this book, I will not teach the physiology or medicine of depression. Understanding serotonin or dopamine, or any other combination of what may or may not be happening chemically in your body, will not change my message. I am not a doctor. I am just a guy who struggled for fourteen years with strange, undiagnosed health problems followed by seven years in an emotional hellhole, before I miraculously found a glimmer of meaning in the dark.

Proceed with caution, because not only should you not expect me to offer an absolute cure, you should definitely expect more pain and misunderstanding as you read. Expect nothing more than, perhaps, a little validation that you are not alone. I believe that knowledge will be worth the pain.

I am an unabashed introvert. Most of those who suffer severe depression also fall on the introverted side of that spectrum. If you often find solace in time alone, you may relate better to my story than extreme extroverts. I can only imagine the challenge and confusion for an extrovert, who thrives on social interaction yet feels forced to endure depression's solitude. I acknowledge your pain in advance even if I don't understand it.

I don't expect you to relate or agree with everything I have felt or draw the exact same conclusions. Your experience is agonizingly unique and personal to you. No one else, including me, really understands your struggle. That is one of the things "they don't understand."

2
Negativity

The glass is half full, if you look at it that way.
Change your attitude and change your life.
Choose the power of positive thinking.

Have you heard this? They don't understand that optimism is not always an available choice. "Look on the bright side!" they say. I don't know if I should cry, scream, or punch them in the face! Every word proves they do not understand.

On a "good" day, I bite my tongue and walk away. They have no idea of the tirade I spare them. They have no idea the cruel lambasting diatribe of which I am fully capable and with which I truly want to retaliate. They have no idea how hurtful, how negative, and yet how true, the words that I don't say out loud would be.

If it's a bad day, I do react, and, well ... you know ... let's not talk about that yet.

You didn't just wake up one day and start to see all the negative. You didn't knowingly *choose* those thoughts. It developed over months or years. The miracle of the human brain enlisted all kinds of coping mechanisms to hide it from your conscious awareness, long before you noticed it—avoidance, rationalization, compartmentalization, denial, displacement, defensiveness, projection, trivializing, regression, suppression, sublimation.

It makes no difference to me which coping mechanisms your brain chose without your knowledge. I am not your psychology professor or your therapist. I don't blame you either way.

Regardless, a voice now rants in my head relentlessly. A screaming drill sergeant, a merciless bully, a total ass of a shoulder angel—a demon—and he points out, shrieks out, every flaw in the world. That's all he does! Incessantly, from the dawn of consciousness in the morning to the onset of slumber at night, he shines a spotlight on every offense that could possibly be contrived. He points out every glass that is, in fact, half empty. He tells me what's wrong with my friends, my family, my job, my country, myself. He highlights every one of my own imperfections. He notices every scratch, every dent, and every discoloration or flaw—in everything.

They think that depression makes you think slower. No, not about the negative! The demon spews insults and cruelties like automatic weapon fire. He's like the verbal spawn of an emotions thesaurus and he launches an unlimited supply of emotional grenades that explode indiscriminately: agitation, alienation, alarm, anguish, annoyance, anxiety, apathy, apprehension, bitterness, contempt, cowardice, cruelty, demoralization, disappointment, discomfort, disgust, distress, displeasure, doubt, dread, envy, exasperation, frustration, fury, gloom, grief, grouchiness, hate, helplessness, horror, humiliation, hysteria, indignation, insecurity, irritation, isolation, loathing, loneliness, melancholy, misery, moodiness, nastiness, neglect, nerves, numbness, powerlessness, puzzlement, regret, rejection, reluctance, remorse, resentment, restlessness, ruthlessness, scorn, self-consciousness, shame, sorrow, spite, stubbornness, sullenness, tension, tiredness, uneasiness, unsettledness, unsurity, upset, vengefulness, viciousness, vulnerability, and so on.

Do you know there are more than twice as many words for negative emotions as positive ones? Positive emotions sound vague and ambiguous. Words for negative emotions, on the other hand, convey very specific, detailed nuances. Before depression, you never noticed so many negative emotions. Now, that inner demon makes sure to regurgitate every one of them all over you, and everyone around you.

I wonder sometimes if that inner voice actually is a real satanic dementor from the world of the damned. Perhaps a demon that failed at a more meaningful target has settled for an eternity on your shoulder, whispering and haranguing you with interminable pejorative doublespeak.

Unfortunately, the truth is actually worse than the metaphor. The demon's voice in your head is not actually a stranger. It's not schizophrenia or psychosis. It's not a literal voice. It's *your* voice! Those awful, disgusting, demonic thoughts are *your* thoughts!

> *What kind of person am I, anyway, to think such things?*

If I hear one more so-called "expert" describe depression as anything on the continuum of "sad," I'm going to … well … I'm not allowed to say out loud what the demon tells me to say because in "polite" society we're not allowed to share our true feelings.

"Changing your attitude changes your life," they say. "Just choose to look on the bright side." They don't understand! You try desperately to have a positive attitude. You rack your brain to think of one nice thing to say, and the demon counters with a dozen instant rebuttals. They don't get it. That negative thought you said out loud *was* the nicest thing you could think to say. Nobody can ever know the things your demonic voice wanted you to say, that you held back. You live in the devil's glass that is perpetually half-empty, not because you choose to be negative, but because you try to be positive—and fail!

They see only your negativity, but that is not the real you. That is the demon, and you never stop fighting the demon. From their perspective, you should just be able to reason your way out of it. *Stop being so negative and emotional!* They treat depression differently. They freely admit their bones break when under the duress of too much weight. They just won't admit that their positive outlook would break too, under enough weight.

It's not even always emotional. Often, pessimism is completely rational. Sometimes depression actually makes you more realistic. They really don't see all of those negative things the demon shows you. If they saw them, they'd be just as pessimistic—just as realistic—as you are. Optimism, and happiness, and hope require a little bit—no, a lot—of irrational wishful thinking. To think like they think, you have to *not* see what you see, and you don't know how to do that. You don't want to see the negative. If you knew how to kill the demon, you would, but you can't unsee what he has already shown you. The very same facts and experiences that make them feel better, make you feel worse.

It's not fair! You do the right thing and it doesn't work. God answers their prayers, but not yours. Friends seem to understand them, but not you. Their smiles seem real, but not yours. You feel the effect, but can't find the cause. You do the time, but don't get the reward. You get the punishment, but you didn't enjoy the crime. The world seems to work differently for them than for you.

Depression forces you into a maze of contradictions, and your logic can't reason any way out. One negative thought leads to another … and to another … and another. You have entered the abyss of rumination, and the demon has won. You can no longer be sure of anything you "know" to be true, because what you used to "know" contradicts your experience. Your experience contradicts your religion. It contradicts your upbringing, cultural norms, morality, and polite society. Experience throws all your former certainties into question.

In a just world, you don't deserve to be cast into this prison with no trial, no verdict, and no explanation. You try to find an explanation, but there is none. Even if there is a good reason to be depressed, that doesn't mean you can make it go away. No amount of thinking can solve the dilemma. No amount of logic can solve logical contradictions, but you keep thinking anyway. You ruminate.

Why?

What else are you supposed to do? Give in to the negative emotions? They say to control your emotions, but the more you try to reason your way out of those emotions, the further you slip into the abyss of logical contradictions. It doesn't matter what you do, whether you give in to the emotion or fail at reasoning your way out, it's still negative.

You are not choosing between a glass half full and a glass half empty. There is no glass at the bottom of the pit. There is no sunrise to appreciate when the top of your hole in the ground is 50 feet over your head. You would be happy to choose the sunrise, but your available choices at the bottom of the pit are all dark.

You must choose between the contradiction of a false religion or the uncertainty of nihilism. Truth is not an available choice. You must choose between hurting your family or hurting your friends. *Not* hurting anyone is not an available choice. You must choose between vile thoughts or vile actions. All choices are wrong.

They will tell you all about a person with liver cancer who kept a good attitude even on his deathbed. They will tell you all about a paraplegic with no use of his legs who still radiates happiness. They will tell you all about a blind man and a deaf woman who have better attitudes than you.

What they don't understand is that it's not your liver, or your legs, or your eyes and ears that are broken—it *is* your attitude. Your attitude control isn't misused—it's unusable. The attitude control in your brain broke a long time ago. A paraplegic's legs won't support weight anymore. Your depressed brain doesn't support "happy" anymore. Whatever happened to your attitude, it no longer bends that way. Pushing it harder in a direction it won't go just makes it break.

Asking me to look on the bright side is like asking a paraplegic to stand on his own two feet. My "bright side" is paralyzed. I can't stand on it. I don't have the option to psychologically look at the bright side any more than a blind man has the option to physically look at the bright side.

In depression, all of the available choices are dark. There may be a bad choice and a less bad choice, but there is not a "good" choice.

Your positivity switch is broken. You cannot choose to turn it back on until after you find a way to fix it.

"Negative" is such a polite word. If any word could accurately describe that demon, it wouldn't help anyway. They don't understand that negativity is not something I choose. Just because the wires in their heads have a circuit for the "bright side" doesn't mean I have that circuit available to me. Depression cannot be described, it can only be experienced. They don't understand that in the abyss of severe depression, positivity isn't even an available option.

3
Judgment

Don't just sit there—do something!
Get a job. Stop wasting time.
Think of someone else, for a change.

They don't understand that your intentions are good. You don't make bad choices because you lack character. Quite the opposite, you strive for higher virtue.

They are not completely wrong. Doing something for the greater good and even just keeping the mind occupied works better than the alternative. Selflessness and productivity are noble aims. They just don't understand that you are striving for those things already. They don't see the inward *proactive* part because you are outwardly micromanaging your broken brain's constant *reactions*.

You didn't choose the negative emotions, they emerged over the course of months or years before you even noticed—before you ever recognized an opportunity to choose differently. Without ever knowing—or choosing—you have developed habits that reinforce the depression. Unwelcome negative feelings bring negative thoughts, which in turn bring more negative feelings. Before it got bad enough to notice, your brain had already begun to rewire itself to anticipate negativity. Your mind and body have started to react automatically.

Certain events, objects, places, people, and words somehow became associated with negative feelings in your mind, and like one of Pavlov's dogs your body and mind slipped into a spiral of reactive negativity, with seemingly random triggers over which you have no control.

To this day, I have no idea what happened in my past to create the association, but whenever the wind blows strongly, I instantly slip into a state of agitated despondency. Often, I find myself irritated and snapping at others before I consciously notice the wind howling. Somehow, the circuits in my brain have learned that strong wind portends emotional onslaught.

To avoid the worst-case scenario, I have learned to close all the window blinds and run to the basement, insulated from the sounds. I immediately immerse myself in a video or a game on my phone—anything that might distract me from perception of the wind outside. Otherwise, either a flood of irrational tears, or a deluge of vile rage quickly ensues. If I don't voluntarily isolate myself away from the wind, and the world, I become involuntarily locked in "solitary" emotional confinement for hours with only my shoulder demon to keep me company.

Yes, I have tried confronting the wind and desensitizing myself to it, but that option is no longer available after the emotional meltdown has already begun.

Would it be more virtuous of me to stay in the world and let the wind continue to trigger an emotional cascade of hatred and rage—to break down in a public emotional fit that I could not explain? Or would it be more virtuous to extricate myself from the situation and prevent the breakdown? Everyone else sees me becoming irritable and storming off to be by myself. Inside, I'm just trying to retain control of whatever virtue I have left. They judge my reaction as negative because they don't understand I'm preventing something worse.

I have many triggers. I cannot count the number of times I snapped at one of my children, or dismissed my wife in a way that seemed inappropriate from the outside. Some random happenstance often triggers my brain's broken wiring long before I notice it. I lost count of how many involuntary tears have been shed. Irritability, disgust, apathy? Been there and done that ad nauseam.

It's easy for others to judge your bad choices when their brains have not been rewired. They assume you make the choice to react as you do. However, once you're already depressed, it's not a choice anymore. Bad "choices" just happen before you consciously choose them. Your brain reacts to a trigger even before you are aware of it. Once your brain has been wired to react without your input, your virtue isn't in the reaction; it's in how you handle the reaction, or better yet, how you prevent the trigger. They can't see the difference.

No one will deny it's a positive reaction when your brain automatically pushes the brake pedal at the sight of a red traffic light. Once you develop the habit, the brain pushes the pedal automatically, without any obvious conscious thought. You have trained your brain, on purpose, to react positively to the red traffic light. Your choices created that habit.

On the flip side, your depressed brain rewired itself to react negatively to a trigger you never chose deliberately—the wind, a certain person, or a sensitive subject. You may very well have made choices that led to the triggers, but not with any conscious knowledge of the consequences.

Braking at a red traffic light is good, but imagine if your body suddenly slammed on the brake pedal every time someone on the radio mentioned "Christmas." It would be very confusing, since you never consciously made that association. It would take a long time to figure out what caused you to stop suddenly and upset traffic for no apparent reason. Even once you figured out the trigger, you would have no control over when other people said the trigger word, or sang the trigger song, or displayed the trigger object. Even assuming you knew the trigger, you still would not know how to unlearn the response. Worse, no demon has just one trigger to work with. Lots of random things can send you down that spiral into the abyss, and it's virtually impossible to figure them all out from the bottom of the pit.

Much more than just the wind triggered my emotional cascade. My brain learned all sorts of triggers, from wind to clutter around the house to specific words and subjects that would trigger a cycle of negativity. A healthy brain, whose wiring has not been altered, has an ability to be proactive that a depressed person no longer has. There comes a point when even if you want to act differently, you can't. Yes, it's possible to make choices that will develop new habits and rewire the circuits, but not in the same moment the miswired circuits already react to self-reinforce the negative.

From the inside, your mind reacts without ever giving you an opportunity to stop it. All you can do is apologize afterward. Unfortunately, in the middle of that emotional death spiral, even the apology will not sound sincere. I found the only way I could prevent saying something I regretted was by hiding out alone, where there were no people, or places, or objects, or words, or sensations that might trigger my autopilot emotions. To everyone on the outside, my hiding appeared an insult, as if I didn't love them enough to listen or share their company. From the inside, I was doing them the biggest favor I could give—sparing them from my demon's assault that they would surely receive if I tried to remain in their presence.

Almost every week during a church sermon or Sunday school class, the speaker, who obviously never experienced real depression, would say some version of this untruth: "If you're not happy, you must have done something wrong."

I burst into tears so often in the middle of church, that I often had to leave in the middle of the sermon. I had to walk out so regularly, that I just quit church altogether. Is it virtuous to quit my religion? It doesn't look that way to anyone else. Is it virtuous to avoid the triggers that will further injure my relationships and cause my loved ones pain? Nobody else could understand that avoiding the triggers was not the same as denying God.

In the name of their religion, they become the very people they preach against—they are exactly the same as Job's friends in the Bible accusing him of sin when he had only done what he thought was best. "It must be your fault," they say in oh so many ways.

They have it totally backwards. Sure, if you do something wrong you'll probably feel unhappy, but it doesn't work the other way; unhappiness does not prove you've knowingly done something wrong!

Have I done bad things? Yes. Am I guilty of sinful thoughts? Yes. Does that mean I deserve depression? No. In fact, for me, most of that so-called sin happened because of the depression—not the other way around.

Could you have prevented your depression? Could Job have prevented his pain? Maybe you could have stopped it at the beginning. Maybe there was some choice you made that sent you past the point of no return. Maybe they are right; it's all your fault. They tell me God is just. What goes around, comes around.

Go suck an egg! They don't understand that blame is irrelevant! So it's my fault! Fine! How does that help me? I didn't know what was happening and now it's done! Do they want to help me, or judge me?

Is it possible you could have done something differently to prevent it? Sure, and if Grandma took a different road that day she wouldn't have been killed in that car accident. But she didn't! It's her fault, but it's not her fault. No amount of placing blame will change it. They expect you to feel guilty for a choice you don't even know you made. How do you repent of a sin you don't remember committing? If I had to live my life over again, I have no idea what choice I could make differently to prevent this mental cesspool.

It's even worse if you did do something wrong, on purpose, and you do believe you deserve it. So what. Your fault or not, admitting fault doesn't automatically change the wiring of your brain. Their judgment doesn't help you escape hell; it only limits your options for escape. You can't just decide to make the past go away. Yes, admit your fault. Now what?

I remember reading an article about depression in which the author droned on and on about how depression is nothing more than selfishness. If you were thinking about others and helping others, anxiously engaged in something beneficial, then you wouldn't be depressed.

What a sanctimonious #$&!* Plenty of people worse than you don't have to be depressed like you. Yet, so many of them really believe that they are better than you, just because you are sick and they are not.

I must continually remind myself not to belittle them—they don't understand. It's not their fault. Before I knew depression intimately myself, I, too, used to believe that it all came down to mind over matter. I used to believe that if I didn't feel happy, I did something wrong. It took me a long time to admit other possibilities.

They don't understand that no matter how much control you had at the beginning, you have crossed a line where your body now reacts without you. Because they can't understand *why* you do what you do, they misunderstand *what* you do. (Simon Sinek, *Start with Why*)

I asked my wife to stop saying certain words, addressing certain subjects, or doing specific things that would trigger me. She didn't understand. She interpreted my requests as arbitrary rules, as if I were imposing some sort of chauvinistic oppression on her. She didn't understand my intent, so of course she didn't stop. She would trigger my depression unintentionally, and I had only one choice—avoid my wife! You can imagine how much that helped our marriage—and my depression.

They don't understand, and so they take offense when you ignore them or react with less than the loving response they expect. They ascribe your reactions to some character flaw, rather than giving the benefit of the doubt that you might have another explanation. My wife believed I was being "mean" and let me know. I don't remember being mean very often. I remember trying my utmost to avoid detonating an emotional time bomb, before I no longer had the capacity to walk away. Once a few choice words left my lips, it took all my willpower to walk away—to be nice—and she interpreted it as malevolence.

They often interpret the best you can manage as a personal affront. You try to defer. You try to apologize. You try to explain, but they don't understand.

When my brain is inflamed and my wife leaves garbage on the counter, I get angry. I tell myself my wife is disgusting. I pound on the counter. I make a huffing, grunting noise, my adrenaline spikes like I'm being attacked, and I turn to run away from the threat. All of this happens before I consciously recognize the irritation. I didn't consciously choose any of those reactions. As I run away from the garbage on the counter, my brain enters a highly emotional fight-or-flight mode in which it becomes even more highly sensitive to the mess. Immediately when I turn around, I see an unmopped floor. I try to run away from that only to see piles of clutter in the corner. I get intensely angry and intensely resentful. My demon starts producing long lists of everything I hate. The imbalanced hormones are firing off all kinds of negative things to say and do. By the time I realize my emotions are overreacting, my brain is already arming itself for a fight that I haven't chosen. For years, I had to tiptoe around the house and try not to notice the clutter. Just to go into a less-than-spotless bathroom, I had to tense every muscle and summon the willpower not to explode.

The demon blamed my wife for all of it. I tried to explain. I tried to get her to make changes. I tried to tell her how to help. Unfortunately, my attempts to prevent the triggers placed unfair burdens on her, and she could not help. My reactions, my criticism, and my demands, from her perspective, looked like a sin against her. When she felt like the victim, why shouldn't she judge me for it?

Please don't take this as a criticism of my wife. She and the rest who have not experienced severe depression don't have any worse motives than you do. They call it the way they see it. They can't understand, and so they will impugn your motives. They will ignore your explanation, contradict your most intimate revelations, and reject your pleas for help. They have no frame of reference other than placing the blame on you. You are selfish, lazy, and mean. They don't have the experience to consider another explanation.

They don't understand how hard you try to be unselfish. They don't understand how hard you struggle to work and not be lazy. They don't understand how what they perceive as mean, is the exact opposite. They don't understand that you experience the world differently than they do. They don't understand that sometimes your mind and body react before you can stop it. They don't understand your relentless attempts to resist. They don't understand that every minute you search for that fork in the road that will help you rewire your brain back to how it used to be. They don't understand that if you knew how to stop it, you would. They don't understand how many things you have tried, but failed.

They don't understand that every failure reinforces the presumption that trying only leads to failure. Every failure triggers that slippery slope into ruminating hell. Every failure reinforces the negative emotion, and every failure provides rational evidence that hope is futile. Every failure reinforces the mental wiring that makes it more likely that your body will react without you the next time, before you have any choice to act with intention. Laziness, busywork, dependency, the silent treatment? Sometimes those are the best options of which you are capable. The alternative would be worse. The most virtuous thing you can do is pick the lesser of two evils.

They don't understand that you make the "bad" choices they judge you for, not because your intentions are bad, but because your intentions are good. They judge, but they don't understand.

4
Dissociation

Isn't that funny? Isn't that great?
This is so fun!
Booyah! Hallelujah! Cowabunga! Amen!

They don't understand that you experience life as an observer and not a participant.

> *Meh ... it's not funny to me. I guess it's okay, for you ... No, I'm not mad. I just don't have anything to say about that.*

Some people experience episodes of mania followed by depression. Some people slip into the pit of despair and never go the other way. Often, though, depression locks you in a straitjacket in between the extremes—more numbness than sadness. Not everyone experiences the same depression, and not even the same person experiences the same depression all the time.

Have you ever just stared at the world as if you were watching a simulation in which you did not participate? I sat at the dinner table every day, looking at the people in my life and feeling that I was not actually part of their experience.

You hear them. You see them. You understand them. Yet, regardless, you don't get to feel like you really belong. They laugh and joke, they cry and complain, they fight and make up. You feign a laugh at the appropriate times, frown when necessary, and lift the corners of your eyebrows to show approval when required—because that's what you're supposed to do. It's not automatic for you though, you have to do it consciously.

You see couples holding hands and gazing into each other's eyes with infatuation. You realize they don't feel what you feel. When you see friends sharing each other's company and giggling, you can't help but notice you don't feel it too. At parties, promotions, and victory celebrations, they feel elation. You feel ... the same as you always feel ... nothing!

If you can't feel it, can they? If you don't feel it, is it real? Because you don't feel the same, their joy seems fake. You know it's not. Technically, you know that a long time ago you felt that way too— once, or twice—but it's hard to remember what it felt like. You remember it—kind of. You used to be a person with hopes and fears, interests and aversions, highs and lows, but now you don't know who you are or what your purpose could be. You observe it all, but the meaning behind it vanished long ago.

> *Whoever I am, it's not me. It's getting harder to remember me. I don't know who "me" is. I don't know who I am ... but this isn't it!*

I would go to work. I would sit at my desk. I would try to get something done ... but nothing. At the time to go home, I would have accomplished little more than staring into oblivion for hours. It's not like I felt better when I actually did accomplish something. I felt the same ... nothing!

I could lie on the bed and do nothing for hours—and, if I'm being honest, sometimes days. I would watch "funny" movies or television, but I wouldn't laugh—at least not for real. Afterward, I wouldn't even remember the shows or the conversations because while I may have been physically present, I wasn't mentally involved.

I gave up any goals of accomplishment. It wouldn't make me happy. I didn't desire the fruit of any achievement because I knew it wouldn't satisfy. My goal was to pass the time until I could be unconscious again. If I had to feel nothing, I didn't want to be awake for it. So I'd sleep, and sleep, and sleep … if I could.

If I couldn't sleep, I'd eat. If I was conscious, I would eat, and eat, and eat! I loved food. At least, I imagined I loved food. Often, it definitely didn't taste right. Sometimes it barely tasted of anything at all. Sometimes it tasted good, I guess, but it didn't help. It didn't satisfy. I still felt the same … nothing!

But I'm a man! Sure, food is nothing, but sex should do it—lust, sensuality, erotic stimulation. I'm a man, and it feels—the same as without it—like it should be something … but it's not!

You know you're broken when you have to force yourself to "enjoy" something that should be automatic—and when you don't enjoy it, the nothingness only reinforces the negative death spiral.

I exist in real life … probably … or maybe I exist only in a simulation that needs to be turned off.

The church says you should feel the Spirit, or inspiration, or the love of Jesus, but it doesn't matter how hard you try, how much you submit, or how much you pray. You feel nothing.

The motivational gurus say you should have hope and goals and optimism, but you've tried discipline, vision boards, and energy crystals. You feel nothing.

The health nuts say you should exercise, supplement, and diet. You have tried, and you feel nothing—or at least, nothing better.

They say you should love others, give something back to the world, or help those in need, but it doesn't work. You can *do* it, but you can't *feel* it!

Your partner says, "I love you." Your mother prays for you. Your children "need" you. Your friends want what's best for you. Your boss is disappointed in you. Your doctor misunderstands you. The experts lecture you. Most people just ignore you. Your God seems to be punishing you ... and you feel nothing.

In your mind, you want to feel what they feel. On paper, you hope for joy and satisfaction. In theory, you believe in service, unity, and community. You can say the words "I want" or "I wish" or "I love," but you don't *feel* anything good. You know what you should feel, but you don't. The result—instead of selflessly empathizing with them, you selfishly dwell on your own brokenness. You want to feel for them. It just doesn't work.

> *I don't work. If reality is ... for real ... I must be broken. I exist ... I think I'm really here ... but I wouldn't feel any different if I weren't.*

I exist without passion, without meaning, without contribution, without satisfaction, without hope, without comfort. The sensors on my robotic automaton body are covered in bitter molasses. It's supposed to be sweet, but the syrup has clogged up the touch receptors. The dark viscous ooze has clouded the erotic sensor and shorted out the passion microchip. The swimming pool of life seems to be relaxing for everyone else, but to me, it feels like the pool is filled with glue, distorting the colors, muffling the music, blocking the rays of sunlight, and hindering the cooling breeze. There is no comfortable bed. There are no consoling words. There is no satisfying hug. I move at the speed of a slug encased in amber, and it doesn't matter if my friend wins the lottery or loses a loved one. I feel the same as always ... nothing.

I understand why people succumb to drug or food or sex addiction. I understand why people cut themselves or self-harm. I understand why people turn up obnoxious music, live in disgusting squalor, or put their very lives at risk for the chance at a real sensation. I can't feel real joy, but maybe food or drugs or external stimulation will let me fake it!

In this type of numbness, you just want to feel something—anything. Some depression is intensely negative and some depression is intensely numb. When it's negative, you wish it were numb. When it's numb, sometimes you wish it were negative—anything to escape the numb.

Even if you can't feel any natural comfort or pleasure, you can feel pain. Pain is real. Tears are real. Resentment is real, and so even though you don't want to feel it, you occasionally let yourself slip into that pit of affliction on purpose. I know that in a previous chapter I said you didn't choose to feel negative. You didn't, not at the beginning, but you can only take so many months and years trapped in that bubble of amber before you have to feel something! So when the negative thoughts come, when you feel the ruminations begin, when something innocently triggers your depression and provides an excuse—sometimes … occasionally … every once in a while—when you are tired of being tired of trying to stop the deadness just to be rewarded with cold, detached, nothingness … sometimes you don't try to stop it. Sometimes you let yourself slip into the pit. You know the pit; the pit is familiar. The pit might be hell, but it is not nothing!

You give in to painful, judgmental, pessimistic, self-inflicted hell until you lose consciousness again. How do you feel when you wake up? More nothing! You didn't know there could be more of no thing, but there can. There is always more—more dissociation, more sluggishness, more indifference, more detachment, more hollowness, more nothing.

They assume I feel what they feel. They assume I empathize with others' good news. They assume I empathize with the bad. They assume I wouldn't want pain, just because they still hope for pleasure. When they say "I love you," it means they feel love for me. They don't understand that when I say "I love you" I feel … nothing! They think we have a "relationship." They don't understand that I have a snow globe—a simulation—and there is a short circuit in my connection to the matrix. They say they love me, but I feel invisible anyway. I'm not really here, or at least it wouldn't be any different for them—at least not any worse—if I weren't.

Depression doesn't mean you don't love them. You do, but they feel something you can no longer feel—something real, something tangible, something emotional, and somehow good at the same time. You want to believe it's real, because once upon a time you felt it too. Sadly, you are not that person anymore. That person died a long time ago. You are a ghost, left behind in the physical world, wandering for eternity and going nowhere. Life is a hollow shell. Life is not something you enjoy, it is something you endure—staring, avoiding, tolerating, existing, discomfort, dissatisfaction, dissociation—numbness.

All of those people you see every day living a real life—they don't understand what it means to be an observer and unable to participate.

5
Overwhelm

I'm here to help. You can trust me.
Just be honest and you'll feel better.
I know what you need. Try this …

They don't understand that you are doing the most you can already. You don't have the energy to try anything more.

In order to function with the illusion of normalcy, I could only accept a few hours of work per week. I had a job teaching seminars. I stood in front of a room full of people and talked all day, answered questions all day, shook hands and made polite conversation all day, feigned a smile all day, and forced a facade of enthusiasm all day. It was like sucking in a deep, deep breath of air first thing in the morning, and holding my breath all day.

Unfortunately, I couldn't make it all day. My associates didn't understand why sometimes I refused to have lunch with them. Sometimes—often—I had to find a solitary park bench away from the throng of responsibility and catch another breath. Yes, I am an undeniable introvert, but that's not the introvert talking; that's the depression.

Rarely could I make it another few hours after lunch. I would feel my facade begin to crack. The character I had to play could only endure so long before I could no longer control my reactions. Unconsciously, I would rush my presentation. I would stop accepting questions. If the demon, or the tears, had any chance of breaking out, I would skip over whole sections of the workbook or quickly make an excuse to use the restroom. Almost always, I ended early to escape the exhausting pretense.

Then I would sleep.

When I say sleep, I don't mean I'd go to bed for the night; I mean I'd go to bed for the week. Around the third day, I would wake up with enough energy to pretend again, to hide the tears again, to emerge from my cocoon and pretend like I cared again. After a few days' rest I might have enough energy to try and consider the possibility that maybe I could do something that might have a chance to, perhaps, conceivably, if I were lucky, show me a potential choice that if I tried one more time, then, theoretically, something good might happen.

Lie. Rinse. Repeat.

Lie. Rinse. Repeat.

Living with depression is living a contradiction. In the previous chapter, the depression dulled the emotions to nothing but a numb, hollow existence. Inexplicably, at the same time, you can be hypersensitive to every provocation. A happy child can sound like a screaming child. A sunny day can be blinding. A loving touch or a kind word can be suffocating. How can you be numb to serious emotions and hypersensitive to trivial sensations at the same time? I don't know. That is the world of depression. That is the world of outright contradictions that are impossible to reconcile. That is the pit of despair that overwhelms both the mind and heart to the breaking point.

The demon thwarts your good intentions at your weakest link. If your weakness is anger, the depression makes you angry. If your weakness is a physical illness, the depression makes you sick. If you have a propensity to emotion, the depression produces more melodramatic feelings. If you have an analytical mind, the depression raises more unanswerable contradictions.

Healthy people lie all the time. They hide their weaknesses every day. They master their urges—at least in public. If people are watching, they only blow up the balloon of pretense halfway, and whenever the character they portray on that balloon is stretched too thin, they find a way to let a little pressure out of the balloon.

In depression, on the other hand, you're incapable of letting any air out of your balloon. You can pop, but you can't deflate. At every encounter with the world, you blow a tiny puff of air into the already full bubble. The rubber stretches to its maximum—all day. You try desperately to avoid any situation that might trigger you to exhale prematurely into that balloon. You know that at any moment, your plastic, public veneer is going to tear open. You've been holding your breath all day, and if you exhale in public, the balloon will pop at your weakest point—your most embarrassing character flaw or your most repressed immaturity.

> *Just relax. I love you. You can tell me anything. This is a safe space. Wouldn't you feel better if you just let it out?*

No. No. And No!

> *I've tried that before. I've tried opening up. I've tried telling you the truth. I've tried being honest. I've tried letting go ... and you made it worse ... because no matter how much I try to explain, you don't understand.*

My least favorite trigger—as if I appreciate any of them—happens every day, all day, over and over and over.

"Hi, how are you?" they ask.

"How are you?" asks your partner at the end of the day.

"How are you?" asks every acquaintance you pass.

"How are you?" asks every coworker, every superior, and every subordinate.

"How are you today?" asks the cashier in the store and the telemarketer.

"How are you?" asks every stranger you have ever met in your entire life.

I get it. It's cultural. It just means "hello," and it's polite to acknowledge the greeting and give an answer.

"How are you?"

"Fine, thank you."

It's a breathtakingly common fabrication! In depression, though, it's a bald-faced lie, and telling it only drives home the point to me inside that I don't actually feel "fine." I am not "fine" by any possible definition of "fine." I have to lie. I have to say I'm fine, even though saying it makes me feel worse.

You have to lie. I don't have to tell you what happens when you even hint at the truth.

"Hi, how are you?"

"I wish I were dead."

You're not allowed to say that.

"Hi, how are you?"

"Oh, I've had better days."

You can't even say that, because if they ignore the hint, you feel ignored. You feel worse, and the balloon pops. If they take the hint, they press for more information.

"Oh, I'm sorry, what's wrong?"

As you know, though, people rarely ask "How are you?" because they actually care how you are, and have time to talk about it. If you divulge too much, they respond with an awkward silence. They say nothing; your balloon pops. If you say too little, they answer with a conversation-ending cliché:

- "Look on the bright side."
- "I'm sorry, hope you feel better."
- "I'll pray for you."
- "It can't be that bad."

They ignore, they dismiss, they contradict, and you pop.

You have to lie all day, every day, or you'll have to talk about it. The only thing worse than living alone in your private bubble of despair is actually talking about your most intimate pains and fears, only to be given a response that proves the "listener" can't understand or help. They move on with their lives, and treat you as if you never even said anything at all. At least if they don't know how I really feel, I can't blame them for not understanding. If I try to share and they remove all doubt, I'm even lonelier.

Or worse, they try to help.

One birthday many years ago, my wife gave me a book about a gardening subject that genuinely interested me—the perfect gift. She chose a book that covered a fascinating angle into my most relaxing hobby—very thoughtful. She chose an inexpensive gift so as to not worsen the financial straits my depression had placed us in—perfect. She chose a gift that I could do alone to ease my stress—perfect. She chose something I would have picked for myself in healthy times, had I known about it—and yet it was not perfect. Receiving this "perfect" gift in the depths of depression felt like a cannon of darts aimed at my balloon. It overwhelmed my ability to maintain the lie.

Do you understand that my wife didn't give me a "gift" at all? From my perspective, she did not give me a "book," she gave me an obligation. I had to come up with an answer when she asked about it. Did I read it? Did I like it? To prove I appreciated the gift, I would have to dedicate hours of time reading—requiring energy that I frankly did not have to give. I still have never read the book, and it hurt her that I rejected something so thoughtful.

My finances were strained. My marriage was strained. My children were practically fatherless. My career was nonexistent. My faith had evaporated. My health had collapsed. I felt like everything depended on me, and yet I was incapable of doing anything more. My back was breaking from the weight of responsibility, and to "help," my wife gave me a job—a book to read. While I juggled dozens of balls of responsibility, quite unsuccessfully, my wife threw another ball at me.

I had tried to explain many times that surprise gifts gave me more stress, but there was no way my wife could understand that I could not handle the "perfect" gift. My wife assumed the gift must have communicated that she loved me, understood my struggles and interests, and wanted to help. Actually, to me, the gift proved that she didn't understand at all. The gift proved she hadn't really been listening. The gift proved to me that I had to endure the pit totally alone. I would have preferred no gift at all than a gift that added to the stress and the loneliness.

Countless people from my church and community tried to help. While we were in financial free fall, the generosity of others provided my family anonymous gifts of all varieties: surprise Christmas presents, food on the doorstep, social invites. They tried to help with advice and encouragement. They tried to help with cleaning, or cooking, or doing yard work. They tried to do the "right" thing as they understood it. Perhaps some of these gifts would help you; I don't know. For me, anything short of cash with no strings attached was not help.

"You sound ungrateful!"

I am ungrateful, but I'm not allowed to say that. I have no alternative but to reject the help. I have to pretend that everything is normal. I have to make sure nobody knows how I really feel, or else they will inadvertently push me off of the cliff they are trying to save me from.

Unfortunately, almost everyone who tries to help, "helps" without ever asking you what help you actually want and need. They think they know better than you because you are depressed, emotional, and lazy. You have no energy, show no ambition, and make too many bad decisions. They know what you need better than you do. They don't understand that they are not helping. They are burdening you with suggestions, time commitments, and obligations for which you have no energy—and your balloon pops!

I am ungrateful, yet I'm also grateful. I am grateful they have good intentions, even if they don't know how to act on those intentions properly. I am grateful they mean well, and sometimes they really help. If you have someone who actually listens to the truth and actually helps, congratulations. The rest of us have to lie.

I started a public speaking coaching business. I am a lecturer, and a speaker, and a liar. I can win a motivational speech contest in the morning and ruminate on my last will and testament at night. As an experiment I've tried giving speeches that tell the truth about negative feelings and depression. The result, the room fills with an audience stunned into silence. I am usually the recipient of many compliments when I step down from the stage. The only time I was completely ignored and nobody said anything, or even approached me, was the time I told the truth about my health and shared my honest feelings about it in a public speech. People don't know how to react to the truth.

They don't want the truth; they want feel-good lies. They want to hear how I overcame my challenges. They don't want to hear that I can't. They praise and validate the person who has already succeeded. They ignore the person on the precipice of failure, who needs their help much more.

Depression's contradictions are overwhelming. How long can you tread water before you drown? How long can you run the treadmill before you collapse? How long can you hold your breath before you let go?

The dam is breaking. There are eleven leaks, and you only have ten fingers. They don't understand that your facade is cracking and they are teasing you with a hammer. They make you feel like a piñata. They don't understand that the next straw on the camel's back will be the last straw. They don't understand that despite their noble intentions, they sometimes heap more straws onto the pile. They don't understand that since you are not allowed to get off the treadmill, you have to quit everything in your life other than the treadmill. They don't understand that just because you are not going anywhere doesn't mean you are not running. It's a treadmill! They don't understand that there is not even enough energy to pretend there is enough energy. They don't understand that you can't breathe. They don't understand that you are drowning, and they are offering you a brick. They don't understand that you have to reject their help or you will sink. They don't understand that advice and suggestions and "help" are actually an obligation that adds to your burden. They don't understand that you don't have enough energy to tell the truth when they can't understand the truth. They don't understand that you have to lie, because otherwise your bubble will pop.

They don't understand that you are doing the most you can, and you can't do any more.

6
Guilt

Lots of people have it worse than you.
You're hurting people for no reason.
Count your blessings.

They don't understand that you know it's your fault. They don't need to tell you that you are failing. You already know ... duh! You know you are causing problems. You are not oblivious. That doesn't mean you can fix it.

It was my daughter's eighth birthday. She is the happiest person I know. She sees good in everything. Life is fun for her. Talking is fun. Playing is fun. Jobs are fun—for her. Her bubbly personality radiates love and joy. She was laughing and smiling—just like a normal kid at a birthday party.

I did not want to be at a birthday party. I was depressed for no apparent reason. I should have been happy for her. I should have been grateful for her radiant smile. I should have been able to join with her and share the joy of that special day ... but I couldn't.

Sometimes when you feel depressed, you just don't have enough energy to pretend to be happy anymore. When others around you are cheerful and optimistic, it only drives home the point that you are not—that you can't experience that same joy—that the universe has denied you the pleasure that others take for granted.

As she started to open presents I burst into tears and had to run from the room before anyone noticed, before I stole all the attention, and before I brought the party down into the pit with me.

> *I'm so useless ... I can't even fake a smile for my daughter's birthday. What kind of person am I to resent others' happiness?*

Sometimes, seeing others' happiness makes you more depressed. Sometimes, you have to intentionally avoid energetic, optimistic people. Whether they fail to pull you up, or whether you actively bring them down, you feel guilty.

When you are the party pooper, you feel guilty.

When others' happiness feels irritating, you feel guilty.

When you refuse to do the cleaning or the shopping or other household chores because you are exhausted, you feel guilty.

When you snap at someone, you feel weak, and worthless, and guilty.

When you stay up late or sleep in too long, you feel guilty.

When you fail to earn a living, you feel guilty.

When your negativity strains your relationships, you feel guilty.

When you have to accept handouts and charity from others, you feel guilty.

Because of me others have to do more work. I live off the generosity of others and take more than I give. I don't have the stamina to give what they ask. My brokenness costs money I do not have. I've failed to keep so many promises. My flesh is weak. I've given in to the temptations of food or drugs or lust. I avoid responsibility. I pretend. I lie. Perhaps I cheat or steal—or worse. I'm guilty.

> *I'm just a burden. They would be better off without me. I know it's my fault, but I can't fix it.*

They don't understand that I know I hurt them. They think I can choose not to hurt them, but I feel powerless. They try to point out all your "blessings." They list everything about your life you should be grateful for—your relationships, your possessions, your privileges, your faith. They are not telling you anything you don't already know. You are fully aware of everything that should make you happy—but you are still depressed. Pointing it out only makes you feel more guilty.

> *What kind of person has so much, and still feels so bad? I am pathetic!*

Even worse, they try to "make you feel better" by pointing out that others have it worse than you. Others have had to endure slavery, tyranny, torture, poverty, disability, and illness that you will never know.

> "I heard about a woman who escaped life as a sex slave. She barely survived the physical abuse and lives with permanent disabilities from being regularly struck with an iron rod. Yet she is constantly optimistic and grateful for her life. Others have it so much worse. You have no reason to be depressed."

You're not helping! I know others have it worse. That doesn't change how I feel. It just makes me feel more guilty for being so weak in comparison. I've squandered everything I've been given. I don't deserve what I have. I'm broken. I have no excuse.

I have no excuse?

Depression shouldn't be an excuse, but it is.

Excuses—

It's so easy to make excuses.

Are you really sick, or are you just lazy?

Is your depression really bad enough that you can't participate?

Are you really unable to function, or are you just using your disease as an excuse to dump your responsibilities on others?

One of the hardest things for me is knowing where my depression ends and where my free will begins. I know I'm guilty, but I don't actually know how much of the pain I cause is actually within my control and how much of it is the disease's fault.

Is depression just an excuse? You don't actually know. You make excuses, but are they justified? Depression blurs the line between what the disease makes you do and what you choose to do. Sometimes you feel justified in using your mental state as an excuse, but often you wonder if it's just that—an excuse. You should have taken action. You should have conquered your emotions and pressed forward—but you didn't. Are you really incapable? Are you really a victim? Or is that just a pathetic excuse? No matter what the answer, you feel guilty either way. If you fail because you're sick, you feel guilty. If you fail because you use sickness as an excuse, you feel guilty.

If I really do use depression as an excuse, it's all my fault, and I deserve to feel guilty! It's bad enough that I don't measure up. It's bad enough that my personal failings have prevented me from reaching my potential, but it's not just about me. I am hurting everyone around me.

> *How much better off would my family and friends be if they had someone who could actually share their joy and optimism ... rather than me. How much better would their lives be if they had someone who was productive and made a better living ... rather than me. How much easier would their lives be with someone who didn't need them to cater to daily whims and mood swings ... rather than me.*

Not only have I failed to do the right thing, I've done the wrong things. It feels like every choice I have made makes life harder for them. It's not fair—for them. They deserve better.

I am a physical and emotional drain. I have been mean, and emotional, and judgmental. I've said things I shouldn't have said. I've done things I should not have done. Their lives are full of unnecessary stress and difficulties—and it's my fault.

They think you're oblivious or they think you're malicious, but they don't understand. You are not oblivious. You are not malicious. You know you're hurting them. You know it's unfair for them. You know it's your fault. You wish it were different, but you can't undo the past. You can't fix it.

Sometimes you are mean on purpose, but they don't understand why. Sometimes, making them hurt is easier than making them understand. Sometimes you have to chase them away, so that they leave you alone. Sometimes they won't accept your explanation or non-explanation. Sometimes you have to be rude, or yell, or put your foot down unfairly, because they won't allow you a better option. You have to make them stop probing, and "helping," and making it worse—and you feel guilty!

Your guilt only contributes to your depression. You can't rewind the clock and not get married, or go back and not have kids, or go back and not make a friend—or not be born. There is no undo button for the things that hurt them. You can't remove yourself from the past and spare others the misery that you brought into their lives. They would have been happier with a better mother, a stronger father, a more enthusiastic lover, a better child, a better sibling, a more thoughtful friend, but they didn't have someone else. It was you. You failed, and they suffered—and they will continue to suffer as long as you fail. You know it. Your depression has caused harm, and knowing you've caused harm worsens the depression.

I either have to remove myself from their lives or they have to deal with the crap sandwich I feed them. Either way, blame me! I cannot escape it. I'm sorry … I truly am sorry, but that doesn't change anything. Sorry doesn't unlive my life or undo their pain. No matter how much they tell me to be grateful, no matter how much they guilt trip me, it won't help. They don't understand that I already feel guilty beyond anything they realize. Sometimes the best I can do will cause more pain, and I know it!

I hate Christmas, and one December was a particularly bad year for me. I navigated the Christmas chaos while constantly on the verge of tears, and my thoughts were brooding with perpetual insults on the tip of my tongue. Were I to try to fake the Christmas spirit, I would have either broken down in tears and sucked the joy out of the room, or responded to an innocent provocation with a hate-filled tirade.

I told my wife that year that I refused to participate in Christmas. I refused to buy gifts. I refused to shop, or plan, or participate in traditions. I refused to decorate. I refused to pretend that Christmas made me happy. I checked out completely and lay in bed for days.

It wasn't fair at all. My wife was doing everything: working full-time, earning all the money, doing all the cleaning, taking care of the kids, and now trying to plan Christmas alone. She didn't have time or energy to do it all herself, and I refused to help. I deliberately made her life harder, and I felt guilty.

What they couldn't possibly understand is that, in that dark pit, sometimes refusing to help is the most help I can give. If I hadn't walked away, I would have done something much worse to feel guilty about. I saw no other choice. I was mean so that I wouldn't be vicious. Depression leaves no good choices. It's either do the wrong thing and feel guilty or do a worse thing and feel guilty. Sometimes you have to ignore people. Sometimes you have to break your promises. Sometimes you have to choose the unreasonable lesser evil because, from your perspective, every other option is worse. Because the lesser of two evils is still evil, you still feel guilty—even if it's the best you can do.

You do the best you can, choosing between bad options. It's always the wrong choice when every choice is wrong. No matter which bad choice you choose, you always wish you had chosen something else. Every decision you make seems only to cause more pain. No matter how much thought and concern and goodwill you muster up, you are wrong.

You are the instigator of chaos and confusion. You are the problem and not the solution. You drag down more than you lift up. You make offense more than you make amends. You aggravate more than you placate. You consume more than you produce. Guilty as charged.

You feel awful because of it. It seems like it's out of your control, but you don't know. Maybe you really are just an awful person. Maybe you deserve the guilt. Or maybe, for some reason, you have to feel the guilt even if you don't deserve the blame. You are the perpetrator and yet, somehow, also the victim. It's so damn confusing!

They don't understand that your excuses already make you feel guilty. They don't understand that you know you are hurting them. They don't understand that every time you hurt them, it hurts you. If you feel the guilt, they don't understand why you hurt them anyway. They don't understand that you know it's your choice and your fault. That doesn't mean you have a better choice.

Damned if you do, damned if you don't. Fault if you do, fault if you don't. Pain if you do, pain if you don't. Guilt if you do, guilt if you don't.

7
Hopelessness

You have so much to look forward to.
You can do anything if you put your mind to it.
Never give up. I believe in you!

They don't understand that in utter hopelessness, giving up makes perfect sense. In hopelessness, death isn't the easy way out; it's the only way out. They don't understand how that feels.

I can do anything? No, I can't.

Sometimes depression feels like a bubble, but sometimes depression feels like a hole. Sometimes depression feels like numbness, but sometimes depression encompasses you in abject hell—nothing but pain, nothing but anguish, nothing but misery.

I will now attempt to describe the worst days of my life. I hope you have never been to this hell, but if you have, you will know that mere words can never convey the immeasurable torment that I try to describe.

Hopelessness is not sadness. The hopelessness of hell is a state of "no faith." I don't mean faith in God or faith in religion. I'm talking about the faith we all take for granted each day. I'm talking about the faith that when I bite into the cupcake, I will enjoy it. "Faith," in this sense, means anticipation of a reward that entices you to act. Faith motivates you to try. Faith in God motivates you to obey the Bible. Faith in the scientific method gives you a reason to try an experiment, because you really believe that new understanding is possible on the other side. You must have "faith" that good and pleasure exist to motivate yourself to seek good and pleasure.

If you know the abject hopelessness of severe depression, you have experienced a spiritual crisis that a typical, undepressed atheist or materialist cannot understand—a lack of faith. Whatever is wrong with your body that can bring you to such depths of depression sucks the faith right out of you. What evolutionists, atheists, and even "evil" men don't understand is that they *DO* have faith. Faith in evolution, faith in science, faith in man, faith in personal power, prestige, money, success, or gratification. They believe in something; they hope for something. Hell is not atheism, because atheists have faith to act, faith to work, faith to try, and faith to exist —it's just not faith in God.

In the depths of hell, that hope does not exist, not in God, not even in materialism. In hell you can experience no faith that your actions matter, or that you have any control over which rewards and punishments come to you. Without faith you have no reason to act, no reason to try, no reason to live.

I remember collapsing on the family room carpet after everyone else had gone to bed. I must have been ruminating on all the weakness and all the guilt I felt, but I don't remember the exact trigger. I do remember sobbing uncontrollably, heaving with every gasp of air. Alone in the dark, I was unable to think of anything positive— unable to love, unable to care, unable to hope for anything good.

The sofa was just a few feet away, and yet I remember thinking to myself that I couldn't get there. *Why even try?* I had no "faith" that sitting on a cushion would actually be comfortable, or worth the effort, so I stayed on the floor in the fetal position soaked in tears.

People talk about suicidal thoughts like it's the worst thing ever. True hopelessness is worse than suicidal thoughts. It takes faith in something to believe that taking your own life will actually solve the problem. It takes a modicum of faith to even believe you are capable of succeeding at the attempt. I wanted to be dead, but I couldn't kill myself. I couldn't even muster the ambition to stand up and sit on the couch. I remember the despair thinking that even if I were standing at the train tracks, I wouldn't even have the energy, or faith, to throw myself in front of the train. I would be doomed to suffer forever, paralyzed in emotional vertigo, even if the relief of death were only a few feet away. *It would take so much effort to kill myself ... I'd never be able to do it.* I didn't even have faith in death, let alone life.

No words can describe the despair of true hopelessness. You have already been drowning in numbness. Hopelessness freezes that nihilism in that last moment of suffering, unable to be rescued and unable to die. You exist, chained in a moment of peak exhaustion where you cannot find strength to paddle one more single stroke. You are sinking and cannot hold your breath any longer. Your lungs burn with deoxygenated fatigue and they are about to release that gasp that will suck in a torrent of saltwater. You have finally decided to give up, but strangely, you can't. You've been holding your breath so long that your body won't let you exhale, even if you try. Your brain is deprived of oxygen. You can't think clearly or make any sense of your surroundings. You can't reach the boat, even if it's there. You are past the point of hoping for rescue. You are past the point of struggle. You are sucking in the seawater that should kill you, but you can't actually complete that breath and die.

You are not allowed to die, and you certainly aren't allowed to live. Hell binds you in that moment of helpless, hopeless despair, doomed to live eternity in utter nihilism. The people in the boat can look right at you and not see you. People are all around, but you are completely alone. You have no breath to call for help, and no hope that they would understand your plight even if you did. Faithless existence paralyzes you in that agony between life and death.

I curled up and sobbed uncontrollably in the dark for hours. All I could think was "God, please strike me dead." I repeated that prayer over and over, but not with faith. God never saved me from hell before, and I didn't expect him to actually start then.

I do not know how many times I repeated my sojourn into that faithless hell, but once should be enough punishment for any crime. You can understand only if you have personally experienced this emotional agony. I would not wish this hopelessness on my worst enemy.

Eventually, in the midst of hell you fall asleep and wake up to start a new day. The torture eventually subsides, in part, but once you have been to hell you are forever changed. You don't live in hope, you live in fear. No matter what happens, no matter what the cost, you can't go back to that faithless torment. You are no longer seeking heaven, only avoiding hell. Stay out of that abyss—that's all that matters. Once you've been in the torture chamber, apathy is a good day. Indifference is a good day. Numbness is a good day.

You no longer have any hope for success. You cannot imagine joy. Even if you could strive for something good, good is no longer the goal. Every fiber of physical strength and every flicker of willpower fights not to achieve the good, only to avoid the bad—and you can't even do that. You're already spiritually, mentally, and emotionally dead, incapable of life, but you're forced to remain conscious. How could physical death be any worse? They think suicide condemns the perpetrator to literal hell. They don't understand that life is already literal hell.

Once you've been to hell, you can see no right answers. There's no win-win; not even win-lose; only lose-lose. Once you've been to hell, there's no motivation—no faith—to try, when you know you can't win. Why start, when you are too weak to finish? Your weakness is no longer hypothetical. Once you've been to hell, you can't trust yourself, because you've proven your own impotence. You can't trust others, because they don't understand. You can't trust God, because He's the one who's letting—if not making—this happen.

Your faith has died. Your knowledge has failed. Your expectations have proven untrue. You have no evidence to support any belief but nihilism. Hell denies any meaning in the suffering. There is no higher purpose. There is no big picture. Does "good" even exist? Is "truth" really objective? What is "right" and "wrong?" In hell, it doesn't matter!

> *I have no intrinsic value. I have no worth. I have no soul. I just exist. Free choice is an illusion. There is nothing before and nothing after. I can't change the world. I can't change others ... I can't even change myself ... I wish I were dead!*

But you are not allowed to say that!

Nobody on the outside understands, but death is the least objectionable choice among all the wrong choices. I'm supposed to say I don't understand why anyone would take their own life. I'm supposed to tell you suicide is the same as giving up. I'm supposed to think suicide is failure, but in my hellish reality death seems like the only way to *not* give in to the demon. Death seems the only way to *not* fail at everything, and to actually take control. The only apparent way to win, to destroy that demon parasite, is to destroy the host.

They don't understand.

Let me be clear. I do not encourage you, or anyone else, to take their own life. I'm merely articulating the hopelessness that "they" don't understand.

To them, you can't make the mistake of even showing sympathy for suicidal thoughts, or you're a demon. "I understand why someone would take their own life," I once said out loud. I didn't know that was such a bad thing to say until I said it. You're not allowed to say that. Suddenly, I became the bad guy for not demonizing suicide. I became the bad guy for telling the truth. I became the bad guy for having compassion on those who feel that way.

Every time I say anything out loud that indicates I don't judge and condemn those who take their own lives, people judge *me*. "How can you say you understand? Suicide is selfish," they say. Any intimation that I understand is not socially acceptable.

If I were allowed, I would defend the suicidal:

> *What gives you the right to force someone to live in hell? You are the selfish one! If you expect someone else to suffer more so that you suffer less, I judge you, not them!*

Unfortunately, as you know, we're not allowed to say that.

They believe: "There is always a way out. Everybody deals with hard things." They assume they have dealt with equally difficult challenges. They will not accept any counterargument.

"Death isn't as bad as you think." Can I say that? No.

"Suicide is not the easy way out, and not necessarily selfish." Can I say that? No.

"I'm glad the person is free from the pain." Can I say that? No.

We're not allowed to *not* judge suicide. Society requires us to ostracize the very thought. The culture forces us to lie. If I don't believe someone who takes their own life has damned themself to hell, then *I'm* mentally unstable. In fact, I guarantee that people who have never experienced severe depression's hopelessness themselves —who I specifically cautioned against reading this book—will lambast me and demonize me for speaking these words out loud.

They don't understand how someone can take their own life!

I do understand.

If they don't understand how I could want to die, it's possible that they are better and stronger and more faithful humans than I am. It's possible that I am lost and weak and lacking faith. Of course it's also possible—even likely—that the reason they don't understand why I would do the unthinkable is because they have never experienced that hell for themselves. It's only unthinkable because they've never been put in a position to think it. Maybe the reason "they" don't understand isn't because you and I know something less, but because you and I know something more. They understand *sad*, but they don't understand *hell*.

Once you've been in hell, strangely, you start to understand people who do unthinkable things. You learn about bad mothers who destroy their children's lives, or deadbeat dads who abandon their families. You see reports of deplorables who steal money for drugs, and drunken degenerates who abuse their wives and children. You see people who lie, and cheat, and rape, and steal—and yes, even kill—and because you have been in hell yourself, you *kind-of* understand. You see their actions, and because you've been to hell, you can now easily imagine the vengeance, rage, vitriol, and desire to cause others pain. You've thought the thoughts, even if you haven't done the deeds. You can't condone their evil, but if they feel anything like you have felt, the squalor, and the moral callousness, and the depraved evil, *almost* make sense.

But you're not allowed to say that.

A good person wants you to be happy even if she is not. A bad person gladly allows others to suffer for his own selfish gain. A truly evil person, though, inflicts pain and suffering, even if he doesn't benefit. True evil receives nothing in return, yet forces you to share the misery anyway.

In the deepest hell of severe, hopeless depression, your shoulder demon starts to articulate true evil—wishing pain on others when you would gain nothing. The demon tries to convince you that if you have to be miserable, everyone else should be miserable too. If you can't be happy, why should they? You can't pull yourself up, but you can pull others down. The only power you have left is the ability to hurt others, and it becomes increasingly difficult not to wield that sword. The dark thoughts that cross your mind surprise even yourself.

> *How can I daydream of inflicting pain? What kind of person am I?*

Wishing pain on others solves nothing, but the demon will not relent. They don't understand that you are fighting the power of hell itself.

It's not death that is selfish, it's life. Your "disease" forces you into a selfish nether world against your will. Depression won't let you see past your own pain, your own weakness, and your own guilt. You can't feed the hungry when you yourself are starving. Depression starves you of love and hope and joy, making it impossible to give love and hope and joy.

When you are deathly ill, dizzy, and vomiting with violent heaving, it is virtually impossible to not be selfish. When your feet are in the fire, all you can think about is getting out. How can you think about others when in personal torment? Depression is emotional vertigo, emotional vomit, and emotional fire. The suffering forces you to focus selfishly on your own torture even if you have done nothing wrong. Every moment you remain alive, you remain selfish.

If you do think of others, it becomes easier and easier to think in terms of pain rather than aid. The demon never tires of spouting hopelessness. Every moment I don't die, I slip one step further from merely lamenting my own pain and one step closer to wishing it on others. If I continue to stay alive, I will start to act on those selfish, evil thoughts and actually take pleasure in others' pain. Which is the more selfish act, depriving others of my life, or inflicting them with it? They don't understand. Suicide doesn't have to be selfish. It's not taking yourself out that's selfish. Taking others down with you—that would be selfish. Evil doesn't care whether I live or die. Evil only cares that I inflict as much pain as possible on others.

Sometimes the sinner wants to die, not to create evil, but to stop it—to stop the sin, to stop the abuse, to stop the hate—to stop the selfishness. When there is no faith in goodness, perhaps, there can still be faith in ending the badness. Maybe, for some, suicide is not an act of willful immorality, but an act of faith—faith that the demon will die and stop hurting everyone they love. You want to escape the selfishness. You want to return to the world of meaning, where you can help others and build relationships. You don't want to be a burden any more. Everyone else should not have to accommodate to your weakness. You are tired of your inability to produce and contribute to the world. You are tired of hurting, but moreso you are tired of hurting others.

I'm hopelessly without faith, and if I don't die, I'm afraid the demon will win. They don't understand that. For those who have already given in to the demon and want to hurt others, suicide probably is selfish. On the other hand, if I want to die to spare people rather than hurt them—if I am actually trying to escape the selfishness—are suicidal thoughts as bad as they say?

Hopelessness means there are no good options. You are not choosing between life and death. You are choosing between a selfish life, or a death that others will judge as selfish. If you live, you lose. If you die, you lose. Worse, if you live—you believe everyone else loses too.

I don't fault anyone who chooses to conquer that demon with the ultimate sacrifice—but I'm not allowed to say that. Yes, I understand exactly why someone would take their own life.

I'm not suggesting that you act on those thoughts. **Let me repeat. No matter how good of an argument I make, I am not suggesting that you take your own life!** I do, however, understand those thoughts.

If you intentionally take others down with you and choose to inflict extra evil and pain in the process, then yes, it's selfish evil. But, even though it's evil, I understand it! You're not allowed to admit you understand evil. You're not allowed to admit you have those thoughts, or sometimes wish harm on others. You're expected to just stay in that hell forever, with no escape. They don't understand that remaining unsinged while in hell is impossible. You cannot fight the demon forever without succumbing to some of his hatred.

There is still good in you! That's why you often feel like you have to end the fight before the fight ends you. They don't understand, and so, if you do take your own life, even in the least selfish way you can imagine, you cannot avoid the hellish pain that you leave behind. Damned if you do, and damned if you don't. If you escape your own hell, you leave a little hell behind for everyone else—because they think it's evil, and they can never escape what you have left behind. You are forced to live in hell because they think it's wrong to end it. Depression is hopeless.

Since chapter one, we have a deal. I agree to try to explain it and say what I'm not allowed to say—that I understand suicide. You agree, if you have suicidal thoughts, to honestly consider the perspectives on life and death, on which I will elaborate in the rest of this book, before taking any actions. If my arguments resonate with you at all, that fact itself proves that deep inside, the good in you has not been extinguished. Please keep reading.

They don't understand that there is no right answer. You just want them to give you the benefit of the doubt. You are not choosing between good and bad, you are choosing between bad and worse. You are doing the best you can, and they don't understand that the last resort actually makes sense.

8
Loneliness

We all experience hard times.
I know how you feel. I've been there before.
You are not alone.

They don't understand that they don't understand. *You don't know how I feel!* Would you take interior decorating advice from a blind man, or ask a deaf woman to teach you how to DJ the party? It's absurd. No one would take advice from someone who was physically unable to understand and relate to you, and yet for some reason, when it comes to emotion, everybody assumes they experience the same thing as you. In their minds, if they have had depressing thoughts and haven't failed like you, that implies that they must be stronger than you, more rational than you, or have more self-control. It's insulting!

> *I wish you could feel the way I do for just one day ... At least then you would know what it's like! I'd like to see how easy you think it is.*

Is it wrong for me to think that? Is it wrong to wish someone to hell just so that you are not alone? Yes, of course it's wrong, but I think it and I sometimes wish for it anyway.

By definition, anyone who doesn't understand wanting to die hasn't felt what I've felt. No matter what "depression" you think you've experienced, if you don't understand me, you haven't felt what I feel. No matter what "depression" they think they've experienced, if they don't understand you, they haven't felt what you feel.

They don't know that they don't understand, so I can't really hold it against them. Unfortunately, since they don't know they don't understand, it really doesn't do any good to try to explain it to them. If you speak up and say how you really feel, you are likely to get one of two reactions.

First, they might assume they understand anyway. They will feign empathy and offer advice. You smile and act politely. They think they are helping, but you know their advice is misguided. They are not 100 percent wrong, but you don't take marriage advice from a teenager living in Mom's basement, even if that teenager *knows* she's right. By thinking they are helping, sometimes they make it worse. If you reveal your true feelings, you not only have to deal with the feelings but you have to deal with the "help." Trying to convince them that they don't understand is an argument of utter futility.

Secondly, by speaking up and saying how you really feel, you likely create a serious awkwardness. You erect an instant wall of separation between you and others. To be honest, I prefer this reaction. When I accidentally mention how I easily cry at movies, or that "I'm okay with dying," people seem stunned into silence. They suddenly avoid any interaction with me for fear that they will upset my delicate emotional balance. They don't know how to respond, but at least that proves they know they don't understand. I'll take someone who admits they don't understand any day over someone who thinks they do understand, when they don't.

Unfortunately, creating awkwardness strains an already stressed relationship. Trying to explain depression, even to those who admit they don't understand, takes more energy than you have. It's like talking to the wall, even if the wall loves you and listens intently. Honestly, sometimes you feel worse when the wall loves you and still can't understand. If your closest friend and confidant can't get it, who can?

We surround ourselves with people we care about, who really do care about us and who really want to help, but don't really understand. Most of us try to hide the truth, because we don't really have anyone we can truly talk to about it. You are lucky if you have someone you can talk to, who will listen without giving advice and without altering the relationship. Whether you have no one or whether you have someone who at least listens, deep inside, you really, really, really wish … they really knew … what it really felt like.

I feel downright indignant every time I read or talk to a therapist, psychologist, or other self-proclaimed expert who talks about depression but who clearly hasn't experienced it. They talk about it academically, but no matter how much they know about the biology, or the psychology, the research studies, or the peer-reviewed therapies, even they—the experts—don't understand. You may or may not have a "good reason" to be depressed, but when your closest inner circle and even the experts don't really understand how you feel, that, in and of itself, gives you a good reason to feel depressed. The loneliness of living in a world that no one else shares only adds depression on top of depression.

When someone attacks a child, and you overreact with more anger than is justified, we all kind of just understand, and you get a pass. When we go to the movies, some people make fun of chick-flicks and others make fun of plotless, gratuitous action-flicks, but the fact that we sit there together anyway, proves we actually respect each other's feelings. When you attend your mother's funeral, no rational person thinks less of you when you cry, no matter how big of a man you are.

But when you get angry because you are "depressed," or cry because you are "depressed" … something must be wrong with you—it's not like your mom died.

My mom died in a car accident when I was young. They are half right. Depression is not like my mom died—it's much worse. They don't understand that it's not sadness. It's not anger. It's not a lack of love or lack of personal virtue that sends you off into your own solitary world to be alone. It's depression. Unfortunately, the word "depression" conveys almost nothing about what "depression" actually means.

I have lost loved ones. Depression is worse. I have been without a job, without money, without prospects. Depression is worse. I have fought with my wife and strained relationships to the breaking point. Depression is worse. I have sinned, made bad decisions, and hurt others. Depression is worse. I have been in so much physical pain I could not move. Depression is worse. I have Ménière's disease and have spent many hours on the floor in so much vertigo that I literally could not stand. Depression is worse. Depression encompasses all of the above, and none of the above.

Depression's world of emotional contradiction can only be understood from the inside. It's an inner rage, but not because you are angry at any specific thing. It's desperation, but not because there is any specific goal. It's intense mourning, even when nobody died. It's having gratitude, yet feeling ungrateful. It's feeling love for those you love, but *not* feeling love for those you love. It's pure reason combined with irrational emotion, and pure emotion combined with irrational rumination. It's both. It's both skewed logic and perfect realism. It's disgust and loathing, while at the same time complete submission. It is disapproval, it is contempt, and it is judgment, but it also makes you feel more forgiving, more understanding, and more empathetic. It is running away even when they offer help—sometimes because they offer help. It is abandoning faith, when God is the only possible solution. It is simultaneously self-centered egotism and humiliating surrender. It is a laziness that takes more energy than any work you've ever imagined. It is overreaction *and* over-deliberation. It is unwelcome discomfort, anguish, and pain that sometimes you invite to stay. It is guilt for poor choices you didn't choose. It is exhausting to sleep. It is make-believe in real life. It is intense emotional apathy. It is overwhelming nothingness. It is a slow-motion eternity. It is a true lie. It is fraudulent honesty. It is authentic pretense.

Above all, it is lonely … because *nobody* … and I mean *nobody* … really understands.

You can't explain those contradictions to someone who hasn't felt it. You can't tell the truth, or they misunderstand. You can't lie, without living a lie. You have no choice but to suffer alone. Only God Himself could understand the thoughts and feelings of your soul but He seems silent as well.

You have no choice but to conform to society. You participate in the family, the relationship, the congregation, the office, the club, the team. You go through the motions that "they" expect, but you never quite feel like you are one of them. You see the way they speak and listen to each other, and gaze into each other's eyes with understanding. You see them experience the security of mutual empathy, and the peace of mutual camaraderie. You can't help but notice that they feel something you do not feel. You alone are somehow different.

Perhaps when you can't exactly conform, you even excel. Perhaps you are in a position of power or leadership. Perhaps "they" even envy or admire your skills or position. Perhaps you have exceeded high expectations and seem to have it all. Maybe you have everything anyone could want—except understanding.

You are different, even different from others who are also "depressed." Even those who "understand," don't really understand. You want them to understand something that is uniquely unfair about your personal situation. You know that personal injustice intimately, but either you can't explain it in words, or it's one of those things you're not allowed to talk about.

"You are not alone," they repeat endlessly. However, one thing I have definitely learned in depression: I really am alone. I wish it were not true, but it is. Sometimes, no one else on planet earth can truly understand the exact complexities of your personal internal struggle. Depression is intensely personal, and no one, including me, will ever completely understand what it is like to be you. Many of us understand depression, but none of us truly understands *you*. You are alone.

My depression gets magnified by three very specific, wholly personal challenges that I have not shared in this book, because I cannot share them or make anyone understand them. You have those private secrets too.

Please take solace in the best consolation I can offer. You may not truly understand my experience, and I may not truly understand yours, but we both understand what it means that nobody else understands. We both understand that loneliness and we are not alone in that.

In this book, I want to share the meaning I found in my depression, in hopes that what I have learned may help you cope with your circumstances. That meaning comes in parts two, three, four, and five. So far, in part one, I have merely attempted to put my experience into words, not so much so that you know that I truly understand your hell, but so that you know that I know what it's like when no one else understands. I wrote part one because I felt like it would be unfair to ask you to listen to the perspectives that helped me, without first proving to you that I know what it's like not to be able to say the quiet parts out loud.

They don't understand that they don't understand you, and for what it's worth, I at least understand that I don't completely understand you either.

Part II: Commit to the Rules

9
How NOT to die

I just spent the last eight chapters explaining how it makes perfect sense to me why someone might want to die. I will not recommend suicide to anyone, nor blame anyone for it. However, death is a *permanent* "solution," and therefore, before I go any further, I must explain the rules that I adopted to make sure death did not arrive prematurely.

In part one of this book, I tried to put the experience of depression into words, so that you would be willing to listen to what I say hereafter. If I have failed to articulate thoughts, feelings, and experiences that overlap your own, I apologize. If, however, I have said enough to convince you that I understand something of what it means to be depressed, please also consider what I share now in retrospect, after climbing part of the way out of that hole.

I am not a medical doctor, nor am I licensed to give psychological counseling. I share my story, not because I can tell you how to fix your life, nor because I believe your solution will be the same as mine, but because I believe that learning how I found some peace after 21 years of depression may offer a few small embers of hope that you can too.

Living in depression's nightmare requires you to follow some rules. I cannot dictate what your rules must be. I can only share which rules helped me.

Rule #1: Death must be the last resort

As appealing as death often sounds, death does not offer any satisfaction guarantee. You do not know if death is in fact the end. Possibly, at death you cease to exist. Or perhaps all your worldly problems remain behind as you enter a transcendent realm of eternal bliss. However, what if, after death, your consciousness actually continues on as the same troubled soul you are now? Or worse, what if the temporary nightmare of severe depression here and now, really does become the permanent hellfire of the damned on the other side?

I actually believe none of the above. I do not insist you have any specific beliefs. I merely restate the obvious that none of us knows the precise truth in this matter. Whatever convictions you hold about the reality of heaven, hell, or materialism, you cannot know how good, how bad, or how painful the process might be until you experience it. Death does not offer you any guarantee.

When you choose death, you gamble that the other side will be an improvement—which is not a certainty. You cannot change your mind after the fact. Since you have no guaranteed recourse after death, reason dictates that death must be the last resort.

I will not insult your character by assuming you would consider suicide on a whim. You have most certainly tried all kinds of things to escape depression that nobody even knows about. Very few of us consider death at the first opportunity.

I tried everything—doctors, vitamins and supplements, exercise, meditation, schedule changes, electromagnetic therapy, goal setting, oxygen therapy, reflexology, enemas, chelation, whole food, organic food, chiropractic, earthing, fasting, social support, denial, immersion into work, willpower, drugs, prayer, etc. My physical and emotional suffering became so unlivable for me that I relented to trying anything—whether I believed in it or not.

I knew intuitively that death should be the last resort. That meant death had to be an option to consider only after all the other possibilities I was willing to try. It also meant that death should only come after all the possible solutions I was *not* willing to try. In other words, before I considered suicide, I had to try the things that I did not want to try.

They say that death is the easy way out, because from the outside, it seems like a quick "solution." As you know if you are reading this from the inside, suicide is not quick, and there is nothing easy about it. It's not a whim—at least not for you—or you wouldn't be listening to me. It usually takes months or years of pain, planning, guilt, second-guessing, rationalizing, harming relationships, struggling with your faith, and so on. If you have considered ending your own life, you have already proven to yourself you are willing to consider hard things, but accepting death as a viable last resort—the last hard thing—means you have to first try the hard and slow things that you don't really want to try. You know that! Otherwise, you wouldn't be here. Otherwise, you give them an excuse. They will think you took the easy, selfish way.

For me, one of those hard things was food. My depression had ruined everything in my life—my career, my finances, my friendships, my marriage, my passions, hobbies, entertainment, recreation. All that I had left was food. Food was my only pseudo-pleasure. Whatever possessed my body made food taste bland half of the time, but food came closer than anything else to providing actual gratification.

To give up food was a *hard* decision because nothing else in my "life" was worth living for. Pathetic? Yes, but everything else caused pain. Sometimes, even eating only added to the emotional pain, nevertheless, life without the only apparent pleasure—food—would be, for me, no life at all. I had tried switching to organic food, or eliminating specific foods, but to truly go all in, I had to commit to myself that I would give up whatever it would take. If my problem turned out to be dairy, or wheat, or sugar, that meant restoring my life had to be worth more than dairy, or wheat, or sugar. I had to know I tried all the hard things before I resorted to the last resort.

In the fall of 2018, after a few months of gradual improvement, I relapsed. My Ménière's disease returned with a vengeance and I found myself regularly heaving violently on the floor with uncontrollable vertigo. On a daily basis I felt lightheaded at best, completely dizzy and unable to function at worst. I could not concentrate on anything productive. One ear had grown nearly entirely deaf. I began passing out and injuring myself in the falls. All of this piled on top of the preexisting depression. My body's physical deterioration in 2018 proved to be the last straw.

I lived in a broken body—a prison—and if nothing changed as I aged, the day would come when I would be trapped in hell and I would be too weak or too helpless to even communicate my pain. The only thing worse than imagining hell was imagining hell without an option to die. I could never let myself get incapacitated past my ability to end it all.

One autumn day in 2018, I found myself repeating a familiar refrain: "Please God, kill me now." Knowing that God never granted that request, and with no true faith that He would accede to my wishes, I decided that I had to conduct one last experiment before I could surrender. I had to give up the pleasure of food completely. I committed to follow an insanely restrictive diet, perfectly for one full year. Either the disease had to die or I had to die. I had to do the one thing I didn't want to do—give up my only pleasure—before I could prove to myself and my God that death was truly the last resort. After one more year, if I failed again, I would stop working on how to fix it, and start working on how to end it.

Diet did not solve my problem, but somehow, my commitment to place my last desire onto that sacrificial altar helped me see a miraculous ladder out of that pit. From the bottom of the pit, you already feel like you have lost everything. Giving up more, voluntarily, seems impossible—but that's what you have to do. They believe suicide is the easy way out. Don't prove them right. Whatever vice, stubborn belief, offense, or self-indulgence you don't want to sacrifice, but that you know might help—that sacrifice must come before the last resort!

Maybe you don't want to try antidepressant drugs, or therapists, or revealing your intimate feelings to loved ones, or spending more money. Maybe you don't believe you can endure a change in diet, or more exercise, or a better sleep schedule. Maybe you have refused to change your home, family relationships, habits, job, or friends. You probably know which one addiction or habit you feel you do not have the strength to abandon. Whatever change might help—especially if you don't want to change it—must come before the last resort.

I committed to rule number one: **Death will be the last resort, only** *after* **I try the other things I don't want to try.**

Rule #2: Give it time

Time heals all wounds. It gets better. All things come to an end.

Yes, those are some of those stupid, irritating, and false clichés that "they" love to throw around. Nevertheless, time does heal *some* wounds. Sometimes depression does get better on its own without any rhyme or reason. Sometimes, the worst parts prove temporary and come to an end. Even more likely, though, more time will give you more opportunity to find a solution. More time doesn't necessarily make the depression more likely to end on its own, but more time does make it more likely you will find a way to cope without ending everything.

Toughing it out appears on everyone's I-don't-want-to-do-it list. By definition, though, death isn't the last resort if you haven't yet tried enduring the pain a little longer.

I know "give it time" is the kind of thing everybody says that doesn't understand. I know you don't want me to tell you to tough it out, and I would be raging mad that someone said it to me when I was already giving it my all. I hope you know from what I've told you about my personal hell, that I know what an awful thing I ask. I appear to be doing the very thing I rail against—asking you to remain in hell longer, so as not to offend people who don't understand that hell. I'm not trying to appeal to the better angels of your nature. I'm trying to appeal to the baser ones. I'm not now asking you to live in hell for others' sake. I'm asking you to live in hell for yourself.

How does more time help *me*? Even at the bottom of the pit, I knew I had to tough it out for a while longer, so that regardless of what others thought, I knew for myself, before my God and my demons, that I honestly gave it my all before the last resort. How much is my all? How much time is enough?

I made that call after fourteen years of physical issues and seven years of mental hellfire. I begged for death more times than I could count, but I refused to take that burden onto myself until I knew I had tried everything else to the best of my ability. For me, it took 21 years to prove to myself that I really tried everything before I allowed myself to consider acting on more dire inclinations.

I can't tell you how many years you have to endure to prove to yourself that you did your best. I can only tell you that my rule required that the last resort could not be a whim. It had to be a deliberate choice, and my expectation of relief had to have a waiting period. I suggest that the waiting period should come in years—not months, not days, not hours. Even when my waiting period expired, that would not automatically give me permission to die. It would only give permission to reevaluate if I had left any options on the table. Usually, you set another waiting period while you try again.

If imagining your pain extending for many more years with an unspecified end seems unlivable, I get it. By itself, this "rule" is a long-term principle, and does not solve the day-to-day hurdles. Nevertheless, you can't tackle those day-to-day hurdles if you haven't first committed to give yourself the time to do so.

I committed to rule number two: **I will endure *at least* _____ (fill in the blank) more *years*.**

Rule #3: Act selflessly

It's time to appeal to those better angels. Those who do not understand almost universally believe suicide is selfish. Sometimes that is true. For example, when I see a news report about a school shooter who feels the need to take out other innocent people with himself, I see selfishness. When I hear of someone who takes their own life in a method or location that deliberately traumatizes others or purposefully adds unnecessary insult, I see selfishness.

Those cases are exceptions. Most of us are not trying to hurt others; we are desperately trying not to. That's one of the things that makes suicide so difficult—we know that those we love, and those who love us, will be hurt. If not for that fact, many more of us would not be here.

I prayed over and over, without faith, for God to end my life because, if God did it, then my kids couldn't blame me. If my death traumatized them, they could not use my choice as an excuse in their own lives. Also, if my death was not my choice, it could not be a mortal sin, and my family wouldn't fear for my salvation.

I wanted to pass the blame to God, not because I was a bad person, but because I was a good person, who really did care how my life affected others. If God or natural causes didn't kill me, every other option I could think of left open the possibility that my kids would be emotionally scarred. I may not be ending my hell but only transferring it to someone else.

I once had a roommate who, as a child, found his mother's body after her suicide. He, like others in his situation, can never leave that past completely in the past. It follows them forever. It doesn't matter how old someone grows; sometimes they never fully recover if they don't understand—and you know that they don't understand. Not understanding makes your death that much harder. It is very difficult to formulate a plan that spares the feelings of those who remain alive—but that is the point! The last resort should be hard! If the last resort is actually a valid resort, then it doesn't matter how hard it is. Whatever I decided, I committed not to do it just for me, but for them.

I understand that you often feel like others would be better off without you. I understand if you believe nobody would even miss you, for real. You may drag others down every day already. You may really feel like your continued life will only hurt people. I understand that your reasoning isn't selfish—to you.

However, consider this. When you suffer severe depression and others say insensitive things and ignore important requests that prove they don't understand *you*, doesn't it seem like *they* are being selfish? When they naively do things that make your depression harder to manage, it feels like *they* are not even trying to consider how they add to your pain. Likewise, it feels selfish to them when you accept death as the answer, even if you have noble intentions. It is one of depression's many no-win situations.

Unselfishness is not just doing what you think is best for others. Part of unselfishness means sometimes doing what others think is best for themselves, even if you disagree. We can't complain that they don't understand us, and also pretend that we understand them. If you want them to understand how the last resort feels from your shoes, you have to try to understand how the last resort feels from their shoes. It's not fair for them to force you to live in hell, but it's also not fair for your demise to create hell for them.

I cannot tell you how to balance that equation. If the last resort is right—or better said, if the last resort is not wrong—then the last resort will be very hard.

I committed to rule number three: **I will do what is best for *others*, not just what is best for me.**

Rule #4: Never make the decision in the pit

As perhaps the most important rule I set for myself, I committed that I would never take my own life at a low point, only at a high point.

As you know, depression is not the same feeling every minute of every day. Depression's turbulent flight swings irregularly back and forth, up and down. At the top of the roller coaster, some people experience maniacal heaven. The bottom of the hill is hell. The top of *my* hill was apathy.

For example, if you want to make good dietary decisions, you don't allow yourself to walk into the doughnut shop when you haven't eaten all day. When you are filled with anger is not the best time to discuss "complaints" with a loved one. Likewise, the bottom of the roller coaster—when you feel utter despair—is not the time to plan your own demise. In the most volatile emotional states, we often make bad decisions. You will regret more decisions from the pit than from level ground.

If you find it easy to plan the last resort in the pit, but don't find it as easy to think about when not as low, that only proves my point. Clearly, you see something from above that you cannot see from below. The worst hour feels like it will never end, but you know the roller coaster eventually comes back up, at least part of the way. The despair might not go away entirely, or even mostly. You might not get off the coaster, but you don't ever stay at the very bottom. You keep moving. We make the best decisions at the least emotional swings of that ride—not in the lowest part of that pit.

For about seven years, my roller coaster maxed out at indifference. While it might not have been an entirely healthy state, I knew that in that apathy I would make much better decisions than in the abyss. I agreed with myself that to choose the last resort, it could only be morally acceptable from the calmest, least depressed section of my coaster. If my life really were that bad, if death would solve the problem, despite the pain it would cause those I love, then it should be just as obvious to me at the top of the coaster as at the bottom. If my life offered the world nothing, even at the top, and I had truly tried every other option, only then would I allow myself to seek the end. I will only make the final decision when my mind can act its most rational and its most emotionally stable.

I committed to rule number four: **I will not make a permanent decision from the pit.**

These are the rules that I set for myself. Please consider them for yourself, and add whatever rules of your own that will help you stay true to your conscience. I will not dictate your rules, but I do insist that to have integrity—to have a justifiable moral foundation to your decisions—you must have rules.

10
How to Live

Some rules, as discussed previously, concern how not to die. You need other rules to help you live.

Rule #5: Commit to the truth

I struggled to admit that my brain, or hormones, or emotions might not be entirely within my control. It took me a long time to admit that I did, in fact, "have depression." Admit it, but only if it's true! Some people feel just routine sadness, justifiable anxiety, and understandable emotional drama, and call it "depression" as an excuse. If you didn't understand much of my descriptions of negativity, numbness, overwhelm, guilt, and hopelessness in the first eight chapters, maybe the truth is that you are not clinically depressed. I can't make that call for you. Whether you are too quick to blame "depression" for your actions or too slow to admit your brain sometimes malfunctions, please take the time to determine what is really the truth.

Maybe you have more control than you think. Maybe you have less. Which is the truth?

I persisted in the second group, refusing to give myself permission to *not* blame myself. I would not admit that I could not overcome my emotions by willpower alone. Not admitting that some challenges were, in fact, out of my control, only generated more guilt and more hopelessness.

Let's tell ourselves the truth.

Let's admit that it's okay to feel emotions. If you have endured a heinous disease, contracted a bitter relationship, survived an emotional trauma, or committed a gross immorality in your past that caused your depression, let's admit that an awful experience is a good reason to feel depressed.

If you know of no good reason to feel the way you do, let's admit that brain chemicals don't always work perfectly, and you don't need a reason. Emotions don't have to follow logic. It happens. Reason or not, if you are depressed, the truth is that you are depressed. That's just what happens when your brain wiring occasionally malfunctions. You don't need to justify it, even if you can!

Let's admit that your life is less than it could be.

Let's admit that it still can be more.

Let's admit that we're not always in control.

Let's admit that we are in over our heads.

Let's admit that we need help.

Let's also admit that some of our own bad choices make it worse.

Admit that "they" will never truly understand your innermost feelings no matter how much you wish they would or you try to explain.

Admit that even if they don't understand, "they" still know some things you don't know.

Admit that it's okay to be loved, even if you don't deserve it.

Admit that emotions are real and that reality is emotional.

Admit that some of what you cling to is unhealthy, unhelpful, and untrue.

Let's commit to the truth, even as we also admit that we don't actually know the truth!

A lot of depression therapies rely on helping you identify the incongruities and exaggerations in your logic that lead you further into the pit. If you don't first admit you've fallen into a pit, your logic already fails, and all your conclusions will be false. Even if you fix your body, you won't escape the pit if you don't admit you are in a pit. You can't escape the pit if you keep digging. You can only accept help if you admit you need help. You can only avoid the triggers if you admit there are triggers.

Sometimes you will still believe lies. Sometimes your demon will still invent impossible logic. Sometimes you will still use depression as an excuse, even when you shouldn't. Sometimes you will still blame yourself, even when you've actually done the best you can. You won't always be true to the ideal. You can only set the truth as that ideal, and course-correct along the way.

Determine to accept actual reality over your biased, one-sided, emotionally tainted, hypothetical worldview. Committing to the truth means that you will change your scientific, political, or even religious views when shown a better alternative, nearer to the truth. Committing to the truth means that you will abandon thoughts, and dreams, and habits that you learn are counterproductive to the ideal. Committing to the truth means that you will make choices based on what is right, not based on what is easy, what is popular, or even what you deserve. Committing to the truth means standing alone when you are right and changing your mind when you are wrong, regardless of the short-term hardship.

You know that life will be less painful by accepting that gravity exists, rather than continuing to jump off every cliff to prove you can fly. Inventing an airplane is hard, but in the end, one hundred percent of the time, using true principles to overcome gravity works better than ignoring gravity to begin with.

Commit to rule number five: **Commit to the truth.**

Rule #6: Take one step at a time

Depression destroys finances. It destroys marriages. It destroys friendships and careers. It destroys health, and faith, and reputations. It destroys brain power, and positive energy, and proper reasoning. It destroys hope, and meaning, and self-confidence. Everything, indeed, begins to crumble.

For a while, I tried to do everything and failed. Eventually, when I admitted the truth—that I couldn't do everything—I had to consciously prioritize my life and quit trying to do things I couldn't actually do.

I quit helping with chores around the house.
I quit going to social events.
I quit my hobbies and personal time.
I quit doctors.
I quit working.
I quit paying my bills.
I quit earning money.
I quit church.
I quit fatherhood.
I quit marriage.
I quit accepting help.
I quit caring.
I quit faith.
I quit life.

People who don't understand depression usually think quitting sounds like a bad thing. You live in their world, so you feel guilty at every step. They do not see that your refusal to spend energy when you run out of energy is no worse than their refusal to spend money when they run out of money. Isn't that a good thing, to not spend money you don't have? From the outside, you look irresponsible. From the inside, though, you simply refuse to go into debt and incur an energy deficit that will have to be paid by others after your death.

Sick or not, you have to prioritize where you spend your limited reserves of energy. I did exactly that, focusing my pathetic, fleeting willpower on just one facet of my life, consciously ignoring everything else—on purpose. Let me repeat. I quit everything else—on purpose. I ignored important parts of my life intentionally. I failed deliberately, knowingly, voluntarily, willfully, and by design!

In financial debt, you have to stop spending money you don't have. Of course that won't solve the problem until you eventually produce enough money to pay the debt, but you have to stop the bleeding first. Similarly, if you are burdened by an energy deficit, you have to stop spending energy you do not have before you can ever hope to produce extra energy to balance the debt.

> *But, but, but … You can do whatever you put your mind to!*

That's a lie! It's not true when a mother says it to a disabled child. Nor is it true when you say it to your depressed self. Physical limitations exist in real life. Sometimes, you can't do as much as others.

"You can do anything" is a lie. "You can't do anything" is also a lie. The truth is you can't do everything, but you can do something. You have to work towards something, and that means you have to allow yourself to *not* work toward everything else. You have to sacrifice much of what you want to avoid the debt.

You might think I should know better than to talk about redirecting energy when you have no energy. At the bottom of the roller coaster, I know you can't find spare energy. I also know that on those twists and turns in between the highs and lows, you *can* muster the tiniest willpower. What do you do with that pathetic, minuscule flicker of will?

Pick a priority and invest in it.

I decided I should dedicate all my energy to my marriage. If I didn't have the support of family, I couldn't do anything else. *That has to be most important*, I thought. I used every remnant of self-control I could muster to treat my wife right—to be the best husband I could be. It didn't work. I couldn't do enough. From her perspective, I was still an emotional liability that hurt her.

I decided to pick a new priority. She really needed me to earn a decent living. So instead of focusing on relationship niceties, I focused on work. *Earning a living will fix my relationships!* Since I didn't have energy to pursue a career and family both, I had to tell my wife bluntly, "I know our marriage is broken, but I'm not going to try to fix it right now. I have to earn a living."

I got a new job teaching seminars where I could choose to work as little as needed. I managed only about one day of work per week. Even that paltry investment left no more energy for church, or family, or leisure time. Even sacrificing everything else on the to-do list, I failed to earn a decent paycheck.

Plan C—I stopped working and dedicated myself to my health. I told myself, *I have to feel better or I can't work.* I tried all the doctors, and treatments, and research I could—but it didn't work. Not only did I not get better, I quit paying the bills and the mortgage, and still had no money for doctors or treatments.

Okay, plan D—

> *Nothing else matters but God. If I can restore my faith, I can regain real hope, and find the motivation I lack.*

You probably won't be surprised when I say that God didn't answer my prayers.

If I put my energy into family and friends, I wouldn't have any left to work or to try to earn a living. If I tried to work more, I would neglect family and friends. Besides, I didn't have enough energy to work even half-time. I didn't have energy without health. I couldn't pursue health without money. I couldn't earn money without work. Welcome to depression's gauntlet of perpetual impasse and hopeless rumination.

When I tried to do everything, I failed at everything, and even when I tried to focus on only one thing, I still failed.

How is this a good strategy?

First, because it's honest. I had committed to the truth. Honestly telling my wife I had no intention of fixing our marriage or earning a living was better than pretending to be the breadwinner without actually working. As much as it hurt her for me to say I refused to address my personal failings for a time, at least I no longer forced her to live the lie with me.

Second, I didn't actually fail at everything. I didn't keep failing because prioritizing failed. I continued failing because my priorities were still too big for my pathetic strength. I failed at big things—important things. That is true. Nevertheless, if I kept narrowing my focus to a small enough goal, I eventually succeeded. I didn't need to commit to earning a decent living. I first needed to commit to working on something productive for one hour per day. I had to accept failure in those big, important ideals and give myself credit for small victories that go unnoticed and unappreciated from the outside.

Earn a living. Fix your relationships. Cure your depression. Find faith. Those goals might be unrealistic when you start from the bottom of the pit. When you are depressed, planning every step between the present and some distant future ideal overwhelms your dwindling faith. If you can plan long term, you should plan long term. If not, plan just today. If you can't handle the stress of the whole day, you can plan the next hour. If you've had an especially bad hour, you can plan the next five minutes—or just the next immediate objective. You will fail at many, many things. However, as you prioritize the list and shrink the objectives, you will eventually find what amount of energy, no matter how small, you can expend successfully.

My Ménière's disease, which can send me spontaneously into hours of puking fits of vertigo, leaves me totally helpless. Sometimes, I literally cannot even stand. Just like physical vomit, when depression involuntarily hurls up emotions, in the midst of that moment you cannot succeed at planning your life—or even the next hour. The whole world outside of your internal bubble fades, and you doubt even your ability to survive the next 60 seconds.

You have to focus on one minuscule step at a time! Objectives always need to be realistically achievable, even if it seems trivial to healthy outsiders. In the midst of a physical or emotional vomit, seek the smallest but necessary victory.

I will make it to the toilet! It's not the American dream, but in that introverted bubble of nausea, it's also not nothing! *I will make it to the toilet!* Whether literal or metaphorical, accomplishing that one small feat spares you from what would otherwise be so much worse.

You have to focus on one step at a time, and keep narrowing that focus until you succeed at something. I don't care if that one step is as trivial as getting out of bed, or setting the goal to "brush my teeth today." You have to give yourself credit for any success. Your brain will never be rewired if you keep reinforcing habits of failure. You have to start reinforcing habits of success, no matter how small.

Don't beat yourself up about failing at the big things, because you stopped trying to succeed at the big things, remember? It's okay to fail at something you're not trying to achieve.

You're going to focus on one step at a time, and only when you succeed will you focus on the next step. When you can eat breakfast, only then do you add one more step—eat breakfast *and* brush your teeth. It will start slow, but the more you succeed, the faster you will succeed. Eventually, you'll be ready to dedicate that little bit of energy to tackle something that seems more important to those on the outside, like morals, money, and marriage.

When you plant a seed in the ground, you may see nothing for weeks. Even when that seedling sprouts above the ground it only puts out one or two leaves over the course of months. When you watch that clock, it seems like time slows down. When you watch that pot, it never boils. It's even worse than watching paint dry. Nevertheless, somehow, by mid-summer that seedling starts to grow exponentially, and if cared for persistently, it will bear fruit.

Give yourself credit for any small successes. I know that at times it does not feel like it, but you know rationally that it's better to make it to the toilet than not to try.

That is my third point. When you attempt just one step at a time, and truly focus on achieving something, no matter how small, you know for yourself that you haven't surrendered. On the outside, it may look like you have given up, but you know the excruciating effort on the inside, even if they don't understand. Even if nobody else believes it, because your one-step-at-a-time is too small for them to notice—*you* will know you've not yet reached the last resort.

You are not worthless if you can't do more. Don't believe that lie. Your productivity might be worth less in material terms, but that is not the same as worthless. If you gauge your worth by your accumulation of failure, the weight will stop you from progressing at all. Nobody invests in something because of its worth *now*. Everyone invests only because of what something could be worth in the *future*. It doesn't matter how fast you move. What matters most is which direction you move.

No matter how small the steps, stepping intentionally toward something better moves you in the right direction.

Commit to rule number six: **Take one step at a time.**

The rest of this book concerns those individual steps. I will suggest possible milestones that you might pass by on your journey. You cannot pass every milestone immediately, or all at once. I will not set your priorities for you. Instead, I merely summarize the adjustments to my life that did and did not help me. I have divided these possibilities into three categories.

1. Strengthen the BODY
2. Govern the MIND
3. Yield to the SPIRIT

The BODY means that if your depression stems from a physical cause, nothing will help more than finding that cause.

The MIND means that if you cope with depression using logical incongruities or by holding onto untrue principles, then learning to govern your mind may change everything.

Most importantly, at least to me, was finding meaning in my own suffering. I call this section "yield to the SPIRIT."

Almost certainly, the diagnosis and the remedies will include all of the above. You start wherever you are and take small steps toward something better. I provide the following suggestions for what some of those steps might be.

Part III: Strengthen the Body

11
Medicine

Before I explain any more about how I found some relief from depression, I should give a few more details about my experience with conventional medicine. You should know my experience and biases.

My Physical Disease

I married at 24 years old, and at that time I didn't notice anything wrong. However, just months after the wedding, my health started to fall apart.

One afternoon I was suddenly overtaken by what seemed like a flu virus from an alien world. As the room started to spin with vertigo, I collapsed on the floor involuntarily and proceeded to heave everything out of my stomach. Unlike the flu, the violent retching didn't stop on an empty stomach, and for hours I dry heaved to a point of such exhaustion that I could no longer even prop myself up. The episode finally passed, and after my wife made it home to the rescue, the doctor wrote it off as an unconcerning virus.

Unfortunately, I would never completely recover. Starting on that day, everything in my body just quit working correctly. The pressure in my head never again went away completely. Many years later, a doctor diagnosed this as Ménière's disease, which includes vertigo, dizziness, head pressure, ringing in the ears, and gradual hearing loss. Ménière's disease explained some of my symptoms, but that diagnosis didn't explain nearly everything. The short list of unrelated health oddities included vision problems, migraine aura with and without headache, dehydration, loss of taste, sensitivity to light, tremors, heart palpitations, lightheadedness, nausea, passing out, chronic diarrhea, hormonal oddities, compromised immunity, joint instability, digestive problems, random musculoskeletal pains, spontaneous weakness, paresthesia (tingling), and more.

Every doctor essentially told me to suck it up, because nothing abnormal ever showed up on any scan or blood test. After several months and years of gradual deterioration, it seemed like I would wake up every day with a new problem. A pain in one part of my body would randomly disappear overnight, and a new problem would spontaneously appear somewhere else. For example, one day I woke up with unexplained pain in my legs. Without any physical exercise or exertion the day before, it felt like I tore every muscle and tendon in the gym. For a couple days, I couldn't even lift a leg to cross my ankles in bed or lift my own feet to walk up the stairs. I crawled on my hands and knees, and used my arms to slowly pull my legs up one step at a time. Then, all of a sudden, after a couple days, the pain magically disappeared as quickly as it had appeared.

My immune system deteriorated too. Whenever my kids were sick, I got sick, and it would usually linger with me for months. My chronic inflammation and even physical wounds didn't seem to heal quickly. I started having dental problems no matter how much I brushed and flossed.

I submitted to more tests than I can remember—MRIs, CT scans, ultrasounds, x-rays, endoscopies, etc.—and they all showed nothing. In polite words, the doctors accused me of being a hypochondriac. "You're just extra sensitive to your body." In fact, once when I went to a gastroenterologist about abdominal pain, I left with a prescription for an antidepressant. I never asked for that drug, and we never talked about depression. The doctor just believed it was all in my head.

As a consequence of years of failed diagnoses and disrespect, I learned an extreme distrust of the medical profession. I essentially bankrupted myself with thousands of dollars of pointless tests and doctor visits that accomplished nothing. Because of some legal and political idiocy, on which I will not elaborate, I could not get medical insurance for most of this time. Our finances were toast. Others' charity paid significant portions of my medical bills, but I still couldn't afford to get the medical opinions or treatments I would have considered if I had the money.

I remember the seven-year anniversary of my first vertigo attack, fearing what it would mean to suffer for seven more. Regrettably, I did have to suffer seven more years without a diagnosis or resolution. More often than not, I just felt ambiguously sick in a way that I could not describe. I would tell my wife, "I feel sick in the head." Sometimes I felt nauseated, sometimes I felt pain, sometimes I felt vibrations and tremors that nobody else could feel. I often fell asleep at strange times and locations. At the 14-year anniversary of my first Ménière's episode, I remained sick. In retrospect, depression in some form accompanied me from the beginning, but at the time, I focused on the physical struggle. The mental challenges seemed transient and manageable.

I need to be upfront about my bias that, in general, I no longer trust doctors. I believe the entire medical profession and industry do not facilitate the best interests of the patient, and medical practitioners usually remain oblivious to their inability to accommodate individual needs. That doesn't mean no individual doctor can help with whatever might ail you; it only means that my doctors failed to help me.

I have learned a few things about my body that I can point to as physical defects and partly manage them. However, I do not know the underlying disease. I know I have some problem beyond Ménière's Disease; I just don't know exactly what it is.

My Mental Disease

I would have thought I couldn't take any more, but I didn't yet understand real, severe depression. People who don't understand depression simply have no perspective to fathom how mental illness and emotional turbulence can be more exhausting and more painful than physical suffering. Around 2010, everything took a turn for the worse. What had been primarily a physical trial quickly became an emotional one.

One day, I woke up with neck pains. A headache wasn't unusual, and like so many times before, I expected it to magically disappear within days or weeks—but it didn't. For months, the stiff neck never went away. As usual, the MRIs and the doctors found nothing wrong, and I knew it wasn't my imagination. Today, many years later, although diminished, the neck and head pain has never completely abated. About that same time, my left arm went numb for no apparent reason. It happened overnight, just like everything else—and surprise—the neurologist's tests showed nothing wrong!

After this decline, I could no longer go about my business and hide the pain. The physical pain and suffering created daily obstacles, but in retrospect, none of my physical challenges could even remotely compete with the emotional contradictions of the growing depression. I became irritable at everything, short-tempered, and would lash out or cry at the drop of a hat. I've already described the hopelessness of that time in the first section of this book. I had to spend more and more time alone. Living a normal life became impossible. I had to quit everything. I quit church. I quit marriage. I quit life. I tried to work as much as I could in between regular excursions into hell, but I failed to earn a living. For most of those next seven years, I accomplished virtually nothing but suffering alone in private despair.

Traditional Medicine

At the bottom of that pit, I yearned for any physical relief from the hellfire. An hour without a headache, please. A day without dizziness—if only. The ability to wake up with enough energy to think about something other than my own suffering—I wish. Stop the trembling, stop the tingling, stop the numbness, stop the pain. More energy, better sleep, better concentration, fewer coughs and colds. I didn't care. *Please, doctor, just fix something—anything.*

In other words, I don't know what causes my depression directly, but I do know that my physical defects and ailments make it worse. I have Ménière's disease, and I also have some type of inflammatory or metabolism problem that goes without an exact diagnosis. The more exhausted I feel by the emotional baggage of dealing with my inner ear disability and inflammation, the less I can shoulder any additional burden from depression's emotional and logical contradictions. Doctors have failed spectacularly at determining the cause, but if modern medicine can lessen my vertigo and nausea, ease my muscle pains, or help me sleep better, then medicine will spare some fraction of mental capacity that I can then dedicate to taking another step that I would otherwise be unable to even attempt.

I found a doctor who will occasionally place me on a course of steroids to reduce my inflammation. During those times, I do feel temporarily better. I'll take it. It's better than nothing.

If modern medicine can't help you either, you're in good company. That doesn't mean you shouldn't try. I know that, sometimes, maintaining the painful status quo feels safer and less overwhelming than taking the chance on trying something new. The doctors might fail at curing you, but, remember, I'm not asking you to hope for a miracle depression cure. I'm asking you to hope for minor relief of any *other* physical ailment—even if seemingly unrelated to the depression. Even if you don't believe in a depression cure, you know that minor relief of something else is possible. You've experienced ups and downs, and you know that "up" exists. Minor victories are worth it.

You wish, of course, to make it out of the pit entirely, but in the near term you must first turn to face in the right direction and keep moving. If modern medicine can facilitate any part of that focus or that progress, take advantage of it. You don't necessarily have to treat the depression directly, because treating any other ailment can improve the depression indirectly.

Antidepressant Drugs

My wife told me often and hinted even more often that I was "depressed" and needed to get help. Of course, I knew I was depressed, but my experience with conventional medicine created unique challenges. My wife didn't know that I had already started new pills to try and calm my emotions. Unfortunately, those pills only intensified the hopeless feelings that I described earlier in this book as the most hellacious days of my life. She did not know why, but she did notice my disposition and ability to function rapidly deteriorated. I was so out of it that I didn't even make the association with the pills for myself. If she had not noticed and commented on my demeanor, I may not have ever made the connection to the drugs.

Because of my experience, I ruled out any further attempts at a pharmaceutical solution. I could not describe, nor could I risk returning to that hell that those pills brought on me.

Some people believe trying antidepressant drugs is a no-brainer, because it only takes a few weeks to see how your body reacts. Various studies show that about twenty percent of people see improvements from antidepressant drugs that cannot be explained by placebo or other known causes. If you understand the risks, side effects, and probabilities, you might consider talking to your doctor about drugs. I make no judgment if you choose differently than I did. I want you to consider every possible rescue from that pit.

I have found most doctors and therapists are generally either ignorant of the alternatives or unwilling to be completely honest about drugs' effectiveness, drugs' side effects, and non-drug alternatives. Practitioners of traditional medicine almost never tell you about important research that shows certain types of therapy and supplements work just as well as drugs—with no side effects. Doctors live in a world of pharmaceuticals, and many of them know nothing of non-pharmaceutical alternatives. I recommend that if your doctor or therapist cannot or will not discuss those alternatives, you find someone who will. When nobody else understands, you can't outsource your decisions to somebody else.

In my case, traditional medicine never did anything for my depression other than level accusations and look condescendingly on me as if from some elitist tower. No doctor ever took my complaints seriously, because they trusted a blood test more than they trusted me.

I am not legally licensed to make specific medical recommendations to you, nor do I want to. I do not know your personal circumstances. The cure is not even the subject of this book. Besides, none of those unnamed alternative treatments helped me. I claim only that "they" don't understand depression, and that medical science doesn't know nearly as much about it as they pretend.

For most people, pharmaceuticals are one of the options on the list to try before considering the last resort. If modern medicine has made a difference for you, fantastic! If you haven't tried it, put it on the list.

Yes, modern medicine has a huge role in depression. However, everything I personally learned that helped me escape the pit came from my own effort, from divine inspiration, or from happenstance—not from medicine. On my own, it took 21 years. Modern medicine is one of the contradictions of depression. For lack of alternatives, we often must trust medicine, even though "medicine" doesn't even really understand depression.

Regardless, strengthen the body with the help of medicine.

12
Healthfulness

Nobody really knows what depression is, or what causes it—and it's hard to fix something when you don't know what's broken. You do, however, know that *something* is broken! Depression is not all in your head!

This chapter concerns only the possible remedies—steps that you might consider—that address a physical cause to depression by improving your overall physical health and strength. If a physical defect in your body causes your depression, any therapy or drug can at best mask the symptoms. Ideally, you will find and correct the cause. Then, everything will magically return to normal. However, even in the absence of that miracle, a stronger body will compensate for any defect better than a weaker one. At best, you can find the cause and correct it. In all likelihood, you will strengthen your body and improve partially. At worst, if you strengthen your body, you deteriorate more slowly.

Maybe you have a nutrient deficiency or an unbalanced microbiome. Maybe you have been physically injured in the body or the brain. Maybe you have abnormal growth, congenital deformity, or excess pressure in some vital part of your body. Maybe you have an infection, inflammation, or organ damage that has upset your biochemical balance. Maybe your brain wiring is actually physically different than others because of genetics, or something that happened in your childhood. I don't know your specifics, but I do know that depression often results from a physical cause.

Whether traditional medicine offers you a solution or not, you can still strengthen your body without a doctor's prescription. I spent over twenty years trying to do just that. I realize some of this section might seem cliché. This chapter covers very common advice. If you find this traditional advice on strengthening the body and governing the mind to be unhelpful, please feel free to fast forward to chapter 17, where my more profound thoughts on the yielding to the spirit begin. For now, let's get these cliché items out of the way before we get to some of my more radical beliefs. Cliché or not, healthfulness belongs on the list of valid remedies, and we both agree to consider all options before considering the last resort.

Diet

Don't worry, I'm not selling a diet. I simply believe that the epidemic of depression in our modern world must stem, at least in part, from something that has changed from past generations. We all know that modern food bears little resemblance to what our non-depressed great grandparents ate. Our modern lifestyle involves processed food, additives, pesticides, fungicides, herbicides, antibiotics, environmental pollution, topsoil depletion, synthetic vitamins, overconsumption, eating out of season, eating more frequently, etc.

All of the above probably play a role. I spent decades trying to find any diet change that would help: no carb, low carb, high carb, high fat, low fat, vegetarian, keto, carnivore, proteins, enzymes, minerals, vitamins, high salt, low salt, no sugar, no corn, no grain, no GMO, no processed food, no artificial ingredients, no lectins, no animal products, more fruit, more water, more fiber, supplements, probiotics, prebiotics, fermented food, whole foods, organic foods, raw foods, no food, etc. I have done intermittent fasting, juice fasting, water fasting, and dry fasting. I have gone without food 21 days, 14 days, 7 days, and 72 hours more times than I can count. I have tracked everything I put in my mouth for years at a time—several times. When I finally gave it my last try, I stopped eating everything except what I grew myself organically in my own backyard. I lost 60 pounds.

In 21 years of looking for a diet solution, I never found the magic bullet. Nevertheless, it was worth it. Changing the diet does change how you feel, sometimes for the better, sometimes worse. I didn't find one food that obviously and consistently alleviated the depression, but many people do, and identifying that one food, or the lack thereof, can change your life.

In my case, I discovered that when my health and mental state got really bad, the only thing I could do was stop eating altogether for at least 72 hours. I know my diet relates to my health because fasting usually makes a difference temporarily. However, while fasting makes some things better for me, it makes my Ménière's disease worse. I know diet relates to the depression, but I can't articulate exactly how—not even in my own case, let alone yours.

In my case, for some reason, eating healthy didn't make me feel better. In fact, I feel the best when I eat more salt and more calories! I actually tried it because my cardiologist suggested I try eating *more* salt. Health nuts will argue with me, but I don't care. Despite what any "expert" thinks, the solution is never that simple. No expert who hasn't been in your shoes can pretend they know how you feel, how you should feel, or how you will feel when you follow their advice. The only diet solution that seems to help me has nothing to do with what I eat, but how often I eat.

If I had unlimited money, unlimited contacts, and unlimited time and motivation, I could find someone in the world who could help figure it out better, but when you have been running on that treadmill for 21 years, you just want to get off.

To strengthen the body, try changing your diet.

Toxicities

I believe diet is a big part of the puzzle for almost everyone, but it will probably not be as simple as trusting your favorite online guru, or doing whatever your doctor says. If you haven't tried changing your diet, you haven't tried enough. Trial and error is hard work, but at a minimum, I recommend trying elimination diets to see if you can identify a problem food group: sugar, grain, dairy, lectins, etc. Also, I recommend trying intermittent and extended fasting.

Elimination diets basically remove foods from your body that may be irritating, detrimental, or otherwise toxic. Finding something that makes you feel worse is easier than finding something that makes you feel better.

In summary, I learned that something about my pain went away when I quit eating. I've never figured out what it was, despite my best efforts. Toxicities come in many varieties: unbalanced diet, over-supplementation, drugs, organ failure, parasites, environmental exposure, etc.

Some toxicities require medical intervention or other forms of detox. Other than those exceptions, you have to change that diet or that environment yourself. The principle is simple. Get anything toxic out, and stop putting things you are used to into your body to see if anything changes. I'm an all-or-nothing kind of guy, and I had most success with complete fasting. Most people I know are more willing to try eliminating only one potential food or environmental stressor at a time. That works too.

If for no other reason, following a diet gives you some measure of control when everything else in your life spins out of control.

To strengthen the body, try steps that eliminate potential toxicities.

Deficiencies

One aspect of diet is toxicity. You have to get stuff out of your body that makes you feel worse. The opposite side of that coin is deficiency. For whatever reason, your body might need you to add more of something that's lacking. Without going into the details, know that I tried more vitamins, minerals, probiotics, prebiotics, phytochemical-packed whole foods, and supplements than I can count—all with no success, until …

A major breakthrough came for me when I started taking hydrolyzed collagen as a daily supplement. Unlike everything else that generated only ambiguous results, collagen made a noticeable difference. My mood changed very gradually, but after a few months my wife commented, unprompted, that I had been feeling better. For the first time in over 15 years, I finally found something that actually helped!

I remember clearly one day while sitting in the family room watching a TV show. I actually laughed. I laughed out loud, as if by instinct—like a normal human. I didn't force it. I didn't pretend. I didn't do it to make others feel better or hide my true feelings. I was alone and I genuinely laughed. The feeling caught me off guard. I could not remember the last time I genuinely laughed for real. It had been a lie for so long that I didn't even know how it worked anymore.

When I stopped the collagen, the depression worsened, and when I started again, the depression improved again. The depression did not go away completely. I still experienced episodes of hopeless despair after I started collagen, but if I have to be in the bowels of hell, I choose to suffer one step up the ladder, one step further from the flames—no matter how small the improvement. If I ever hint to my wife that I might run out of collagen, her adrenaline spikes for fear of what will happen, and she insists I'm never allowed to stop taking it.

Before collagen, I kept slipping deeper and deeper. Collagen didn't take me out of the pit, but it did change the direction I was moving. For the first time in years, on some days I actually felt like I could do more. For the first time in a long time, I actually considered committing to new responsibilities. I thank God that somehow I was inspired to try those collagen supplements. It took several years before I saw the level ground at the top of the hole, but collagen lifted me up that first step of the ladder.

Without going into all the nit-picky biology, I must warn you that collagen can have the exact opposite effect of SSRI drugs on the body's serotonin. Collagen may react unpredictably with your internal biology, especially if you are already taking antidepressant drugs. Collagen can also affect cortisol and inflammation in your body. I advise you to consult a doctor who understands the interactions before applying anything I say to your own situation.

I believe the effect of collagen was, for me, more about some congenital protein or enzyme deficiency in my body rather than its effect on serotonin. Something that I don't understand about my body's soft tissue—collagen—relates to my moods. I didn't achieve the ideal and find the root cause of my depression, but I did try one step at a time enough times to find something that strengthened my body just enough to start climbing out of the pit.

Collagen probably won't help you. I'm suggesting, rather, that something tangible can do for you what collagen did for me. Is there something your body needs that it's lacking? What is your deficiency? What is your collagen?

To strengthen the body, try steps that add resources to your body.

Exercise

I am so sick of people who are "healthy" by their own standards, telling me how they never get sick and feel great because of their diet, their workout routine, or their discipline. A change in diet and exercise is probably NOT the solution. It's probably not that easy, but you would be lying to yourself to consider the last resort without trying it.

"You have to do hard things. You have to do things you don't want to do," they say. A depressed person understands this on a level a healthy person can never understand. Every minute of every day of depression we do things we don't want to do. Frankly, the fact that we manage to accomplish as much as we do is amazing. Healthy people from the outside can't see that we *are* doing hard things. They just don't understand.

I know discipline. I know exercise, and it didn't help me. I have done cardio. I have done weights. I have been weak and I have been strong. I've put in the time. I've put in the effort. I've put in the discipline. I've worked up to doing 120 sit-ups, 100 push-ups, 20 pull-ups, walking 20 miles, running five miles. Athletes will think that's nothing, but when you would rather be dead—it's a lot! I've accomplished strength and endurance goals I never dreamed possible—and I hated every minute of it.

Neither light workouts nor heavy workouts made me feel any better. I felt more heart palpitations. In fact, I felt more shakiness. I felt more pain. I felt more lightheadedness, nausea, and dizziness. I felt more depressed. The blood tests and the doctors continued to show nothing.

> *Stop telling me nothing is wrong just because* you *don't know what it is!*

I do usually feel "better" when I occupy my time at some productive effort. Engaging in physical work and moving your body provides a needed distraction. Nevertheless, feeling better doesn't mean the depression goes away. It just means that when you're on the upswing of the roller coaster, a little bit of distraction might help you not dwell on the pain. I include this section because research shows that exercise has been shown to help a lot of people with depression feel better. We all know exercise is good. If exercise helps you feel better, do it!

If you haven't tried it, then don't tell me you are considering the last resort. I know exactly how impossible it seems to expend the kind of energy that exercise requires. When I make these long lists of things I've tried, it might sound like I couldn't have been depressed, because someone with depression could never have the energy to do all that stuff. Remember, this all happened over 21 years! I took only one step at a time, and that only by sacrificing everything else. I am not asking you to try anything I didn't try. I understand if you can't do *more*, but you can do *differently*.

I hated it, but was it worth it? Yes, because I discovered that—*for me*—exercise makes everything worse! I learned that in my body, taxing even a single muscle group to exhaustion means the next day I will not be able to control my emotions. Something in the breakdown and repair process of my body is broken, and somehow it connects to my moods. Because I tried it and gave it my all, I learned to *stop* exercising. I now stay active only in projects with less intensity, mostly gardening-related. I am careful never to push it to the point that any muscle nears the point of exhaustion. I can actively engage in something meaningful, but I can't "exercise."

Perhaps more exercise will make you feel worse too. Or maybe more exercise will make you feel better. Maybe more intense, less intense, less frequent, more frequent, or exercise of a different type will change your life. I cannot guarantee that exercise will make you feel *better*, but I can virtually guarantee that exercise will make you feel *different*. You cannot know how until you try.

To strengthen the body, try steps that change the way you move and exercise.

Respite

One of your tiny successes must be respite: downtime and relaxation. Medically speaking, you need good sleep and a well-timed circadian rhythm to be healthy, obviously. If you don't sleep or can't sleep, that is something you can discuss with your doctor. In addition to sleep, however, you need respite.

You have to not only rest while you are asleep, but recharge while you are awake. The idea that you have to participate in every activity, agree to every conversation, or be an extrovert is not only untrue; it is counterproductive. Whatever your priority, you have to be able to say no to everything that diverts your energy in unhelpful directions. Learn to say no, and then learn to say yes to something that helps. Because you can never completely avoid that energy drain, you have to have somewhere to go or something to do that releases some stress. For me, gardening recharges the battery.

I understand that in the depths of hell, you don't even care about what you want to care about. At my worst, I gave up gardening for years. I knew the real me cared about it deeply, but the depressed me couldn't manage to do anything about it. In fact, thinking about how I didn't care about the things I used to care about gave me even more reason to feel more depressed. I get that respite might not be the next step, but it's one of the crucial steps.

Respite provides a recharge, or at a minimum, stops the discharge. It might be time alone or time with others. It might be work or play. It might be active or inactive. Do something that recharges the battery, even at the expense of what others think matters more, because every extra hint of energy helps you take on the next step and increases the odds of success.

To strengthen the body, find your respite.

Healthful lifestyle changes must not be overlooked. I encourage you to never stop looking for a physical, bodily solution, no matter how many dozens or hundreds of other things you have tried and failed. Strengthen the body by improving health.

13
Alternatives

I learned that the root cause of my problems had to be some physical defect in my metabolism. If left undiscovered, physical defects only lead to more physical weakness, which leads to a vicious cycle of more defects. The sooner you identify any personal physical abnormalities, the better.

Unfortunately, in my case, traditional medicine never found any such defect or diagnosis. If traditional medicine can ease any of your physical symptoms, congratulations! If not, consider the alternatives. Remember, we are not necessarily seeking an absolute cure, just anything that will strengthen the body as a whole. Many holistic and alternative medicine techniques purport to do just that.

Upper Cervical Chiropractic

Having no success with conventional medicine, I began to allocate every spare penny to investigating alternative procedures that, a few years earlier, I would have considered quackery.

I discovered my second miracle through chiropractic care. I had so many doctors tell me, point blank, that chiropractic adjustments don't work that I quit even telling them I had success with chiropractic. Many in the medical community claim chiropractors are quacks or scam artists. I will not dispute that. A lot of chiropractors *are* scam artists. A lot of medical doctors are scam artists, too. I wouldn't judge an entire race because of the idiosyncrasies of one man, nor will I malign an entire profession on the basis of one chiropractor's lack of ethics. I distrust everyone equally.

In the pit, however, you reach a point where you don't care what anybody thinks, or whether or not your doctor agrees, or even if it's dangerous. You just have to get out of that pit at any cost. When ending life sounds better than living life, what your doctor thinks about chiropractors doesn't matter.

Twice over the decades, I spent months visiting a chiropractor regularly with no results other than an empty wallet. Chiropractic didn't work for me, at first. However, in late 2018, I reached one of the lowest points of my life. Collagen had helped for a while, but because of my fasting and dieting, my Ménière's disease had worsened. The buzzing in my ear had become constant, even though the ear itself remained virtually deaf on that side. The dizziness and malaise followed me so often that half of the time I couldn't even read my phone in bed, let alone sit up and work. Despite the emotional improvements from the collagen, my Ménière's disease episodes had become a trigger that sent me regularly slipping back into depression's abyss. The dizzier I became from my inner ear damage, the more frequently my demons enticed me back into the hopelessness of hell. I had only a couple of months earlier concluded that I would give it one more year before I considered the last resort.

Somehow, in my despair, in what I believe came as a flash of divine inspiration, I stumbled across an internet reference to some Ménière's disease sufferers having success with "upper cervical chiropractic." I never considered that different chiropractors had different specialties and training. It turned out that the chiropractors I had visited previously, despite their claim to correct the upper cervical spine, were not, in fact, "upper cervical chiropractors" in the sense of training in that specialty.

I found an upper cervical chiropractor a few miles from my home, and my life has never been the same. My new chiropractor took imaging that showed my top two vertebrae were respectively 6 and 12 degrees out of alignment. It may not sound like much, but many people experience strange symptoms with less than a one-degree misalignment.

How did none of the doctors, CT scans, or MRIs ever find this misalignment? They were not looking. My nephrologist was looking at the kidney test. My gastroenterologist was trying to help with abdominal pain. My neurologist was testing my numb arm. My ENT assumed the dizziness was from Ménière's because that was his specialty, and my cardiologist assumed it was related to blood pressure because that was his specialty. I am not sure why the radiologist didn't notice. It seems like they all see only what they are looking for and discount any other alternatives. They seem to unanimously agree, though, that "chiropractic doesn't work."

It turns out, doctors don't know what they don't know.

A lot of chiropractors get a bad rap because they expect you to come in every week, forever. Yeah, that might be a scam. My new chiropractor, though, expected to see me every week for a few months, and then he expected only rare follow ups. He was actually surprised when I got worse before I got better.

By helping me continue treatment when I was ready to give up, my chiropractor saved my life. It took me months to find confidence that the subtle changes in my symptoms actually resulted from the changes to my neck alignment, but eventually, I became convinced. After a few months, I could finally detect how my symptoms changed by the hour, depending on the juxtaposition of my upper vertebrae. I initially visited the chiropractor with hopes of relieving symptoms of my Ménière's disease, but the treatment actually affected all of my other weird symptoms too—including depression. My atlas vertebra became like a depression on-off switch. If it slipped back six degrees to the right, my shoulder demon shouted obscenities and hatred for everything and everybody. I lived on edge and burst into tears at the drop of a hat. If the chiropractor turned my atlas vertebra six degrees back to the left, where it belonged, the demon left me alone.

As my neck vertebrae moved from one position to another, dizziness and nausea would turn on, muscle pains would appear, and digestion would change. After another adjustment, hot flashes and migraines. The next visit created heart palpitations. One week, diarrhea; the next week, hormonal surprise. I never knew what to expect the days after I left the chiropractor's office. I actually feared the visits because often things got worse before they got better. Nevertheless, the fact that my mysterious symptoms changed whenever my neck alignment changed proved to me that many of my symptoms were related to my neck.

Most people, according to my chiropractor, maintain their neck adjustments more persistently within a few months. It took me two and one-half years before my neck decided to let me relax more than a few days at a time.

In the process of those years, my dehydration is gone. My bowels are normal and regular. My numbness has decreased. Body pains have become understandable rather than random. Heart rate and blood pressure have normalized. My Ménière's disease has subsided, tinnitus diminished. My vertigo episodes last seconds or minutes rather than hours or weeks. I have not passed out in years. I can usually work for hours before I get too tired, and I have undertaken projects to actually contribute to the world.

Did adjusting my neck cure my depression? Cure? No, not completely, but I can say this much: I no longer wish I were dead.

I have talked to an orthopedist who is one of the world's foremost specialists on instability of the upper cervical spine. He noticed a peculiarity on my MRI—either some injury or inflammation on my neck—that he hadn't ever seen before on thousands of other people's necks. He still could not explain my exact symptoms, especially not how cervical misalignment would cause my depression. He told me that's not a common symptom.

They just don't understand depression! No one really understands. No one has truly offered me a satisfactory explanation of my "problem." I cannot explain definitively how or why it works. I know only that when my neck stays aligned properly, the demon dies.

A nationwide directory of upper cervical chiropractors can be found at UpperCervicalCare.com. My chiropractor's specialty is called "advanced orthogonal." My chiropractor receives referrals from medical doctors and refers patients to orthopedists, when necessary. I prefer the philosophy of "alternative medicine" when it works in cooperation with licensed medical doctors, not against them.

Your depression may or may not relate to your neck. My chiropractor came as a miracle sent from God. I cannot promise you that miracle, but I share my experience in case you choose to rule out the possibility. Every straw you remove from the camel's back is one step further from the final straw that breaks it.

Alternative Medicine

My point is not to prescribe upper cervical chiropractic. My point is that a physical defect in your body can lead to more weakness and more problems. Some amino acid or enzyme deficiency in my body led to some ligament weaknesses, which, in turn, created vertebral instability, which led to all kinds of symptoms for me, which overburdened my emotions to the point that I couldn't do anything but stare into the abyss as my depression continually worsened. When you strengthen your body, you might not immediately get out of the pit, but you might be able to change which direction you are facing and at least notice the light at the top of the pit.

Whether or not traditional medicine can help you, there are countless forms of alternative medicine: cleansing, acupuncture, prayer, meditation, kinesiology, aromatherapy, massage therapy, light therapy, electromagnetic therapy, oxygen therapy, cryogenics, homeopathy, hypnosis, NLP, reflexology, earthing, and countless other alternatives—some with and some without scientific support. I'm not recommending you put faith in pseudoscience. I'm asking you, before the last resort, not to ignore anything that you believe might strengthen your body and free up the energy to move forward to the next step.

To strengthen the body, try alternative medicine.

Remedies

I use the word "remedy" liberally. I am not cured. Whatever happened to my brain and body over the last two decades of emotional vertigo will never be completely erased. My brain cannot compute as fast as it used to. The combination of age and depression has made it impossible to continue with the mental tasks and concentration that used to be second nature. Worse, the wiring of my brain adapted over the years to respond negatively to unexpected triggers, and that cannot be unwired easily. Depression permanently changed me physically. I can never again be the person I was before. Any "remedy" to depression yields only a partial restoration. You can't un-live the experience and unmake the choices, or undo the damage you made while in the pit. I'm still broken and often exhausted, dizzy, and in pain. I'm still not usually "happy." I haven't yet restored the habits of sleep, and work, and relationships that healthy people take for granted. I have not restored the optimism, certainty, or faith on which I used to rely.

By many standards, I'm still depressed, but inside, it's me. My inner voice is not a stranger that I don't recognize, and it's not nothing—it's me. It's nice to be here again. I really missed myself.

Depression is not all in your head, no matter who says differently, no matter what degrees they flaunt, no matter what spiritual insight they claim. Sometimes depression has a real, physical cause and a real, physical solution. No matter how else you cope in the meantime, never stop looking for a physical cause. If you don't find that underlying cause, strengthen your body anyway.

Strengthen the body with medicine, with healthfulness, and with any alternative remedy that helps. Worst case, you get worse slower. Best case, you get better. Strengthen the body!

Part IV: Govern the Mind

14
Cooperation

Physical cause or not, when you believe lies you start to feel depressed, and when you become depressed you start to believe more lies. "I *can't* do anything" is just as big of a lie as "You *can* do anything." Similarly, "Give up" is just as big of a lie as "Tough it out." Everything is not your fault, nor is everything beyond your control. Depression often has physical causes, as discussed in the previous chapters. However, depression also comes from false and irrational—or at least unhelpful—thinking.

Someone who has not experienced real depression probably will not understand that "I can't" is not necessarily an excuse. Nevertheless, there is a fine line between saying "I can't" and saying "I won't," and unfortunately, sometimes it's hard to tell the difference. In yet one more ironic contradiction, depression is a real excuse, and yet you can't use it as an excuse, because you can't know the excuse is real. Once depression becomes an excuse, more and more of what actually is within your control gets blamed on the depression, and the emotions only spiral deeper into the abyss.

How can you accept that you are susceptible to a real disease, and yet not use it as an excuse? This section of the book, part four, briefly addresses steps that might improve that unhelpful thinking and better govern your mind. The first change of mind involves the nature of your relationships to others. Is it competition or cooperation?

Seek Cooperation

Competition will restrain your progress, perhaps more than any other lie. The culture in which we live almost certainly pressures you to climb the ladder of success, to outdo others, to be in charge, to prove your physical prowess, your emotional control, or your moral and ethical virtue. Stop it!

Why do you have to prove yourself? Why do you have to climb higher up the mountain than someone else? Why do you have to be more virtuous than your friends or family members? Why do you have to make more money? Why do you have to be more popular? Why do you need more friends or more influence? Why do you have to be better than others? Why?

You know you are not. Your demon tells you all the time that you are not—that you are not doing enough. You cannot believe both things. You cannot believe you are depressed and incapable of more, too exhausted to tackle the world, worthless, overwhelmed, and guilty ... *and* believe you must be better than others. Talk about a recipe for depression!

There is nothing wrong with being below average. There is nothing ethically suspect about being not as good or further behind in the race. As long as you are still moving in the right direction, failure to finish the race first is not a moral failing, just a circumstantial one. Who deserves more respect: the imbecile who moves in the right direction, progressing gradually behind the pack, or the gifted and talented paragon of virtue in front of the line whose life gradually deteriorates from inaction? Who is the moral superior: the hypocrite who says the right things and looks the right way and receives public acclaim, or the one who actually believes the right things and acts with noble intentions without it? Failing more often than you want doesn't prove anything other than the fact that you haven't stopped trying. Those who try more, fail more. Those who fail the most probably tried the most. Comparing your private tally of personal failure to another's list of public success is an impossible proposition. You know everything on your list of failure, and nothing on theirs. You cannot win that competition.

Don't seek competition. Seek cooperation. Change your mind. Change your expectation. Change the goal.

If your fellow humans judge you for your disease, ridicule you for failure, and dismiss your pain, they are not "on your team." Why should you accept their worldview, when they are not even on your team? The uncooperative are not teammates. They are not companions; they are competitors. If they see themselves as superiors because they have been spared your challenges, they believe a lie. You don't have to walk off that cliff with them. You don't have to take others' need for competition as a statement about your own worth. Don't let your competitors choose your path. If they think life is a competition to win or lose, then what they tell you to do is guaranteed to help them feel superior, not help you. If you accept their worldview, you automatically lose by their standard.

Others may very well be superior at earning money, or being happy, or staying busy, but you know things they don't know. Depression needs not a competitor but a companion—someone who wants to share all they have and lift you up, not someone who revels in the comparison that gives them a higher status.

Finding real, non-competitive companionship seems impossible, because all depression produces loneliness. You can't feel like you have real companionship when they don't understand. Hopefully, you have someone who will listen to you and give you the benefit of the doubt without unsolicited advice and judgment. Unfortunately, because they don't understand, most of us don't have someone who fills that need.

Without a true nonjudgmental, longsuffering companion, you have to find some common goal or activity that unifies you with others, based on what you share, not based on how you compare. Competition takes too much energy. You don't need to climb the ladder over anyone else spiritually, politically, financially, morally, or otherwise nearly as much as you need someone to share your rung of the ladder.

If you can't yet find intimate soul searching companionship, please seek plain old ordinary cooperation. Cooperation can include sharing your respite, hobbies, playing games, visiting family, church, work, diet or exercise groups, talking to a cashier at the supermarket, or anything in between. Especially for introverts, depression leads you to do things in more isolation, more often alone, and less publicly. Because they don't understand, yielding to that impulse makes sense—but it doesn't work.

You have to find something you can share with other people. Only you know what that topic of discussion, activity, or noble cause can be. Find a time and place to participate in a no-lose, non-competitive interaction. Participate in something where you can interact with others with no competitive strings attached. When they try to attach competitive strings, commit to the truth and refuse.

Cooperation must be one of the steps on your path because depression feels isolating and rewires the brain to reinforce that expectation. To unwire that habit, you have to enter the world of real human interaction one step at a time.

To govern the mind, find non-competitive relationships.

Forgive Yourself

If you haven't abandoned competition in favor of cooperation, you probably haven't forgiven yourself. You don't forgive yourself because you are comparing yourself to others and you feel like less. Or worse, you think you're more and don't need to forgive yourself. Either way, you are looking at life as a competition.

Almost certainly, either you hurt people and that contributed to the depression, or the depression contributed to you hurting people. Either way you feel guilty. You must forgive yourself for failing, even if you have hurt others. You can't cooperate effectively when you consistently compare your moral virtue to theirs. It's okay if they are better than you. How are they supposed to help you if they don't have something you do not?

When you stop trying to be the perfect woman, you can stop blaming yourself for being an imperfect woman. When you stop trying to be the perfect man, you can stop blaming yourself for being an imperfect man. Someday you will work on that. You don't have to feel guilty about it until that is the next step on the path. Don't feel guilty for failing to run while you are still re-learning to walk.

You know all of those things you've done that may have caused your depression? You know those awful, seemingly unforgivable transgressions? So what. I forgive you, because you can't do anything about it now. The thief can't give me back my money when he's unconscious in the hospital with a gunshot wound. You've done a lot of things that hurt people. Forgive yourself, even if they don't forgive you. Whether you can ever fix it or not, you can't fix it when you're dead.

If you believe in Jesus, pray and ask that God take the burden from you. If you don't believe in God, pray anyway, and ask that the burden be forgiven. You might not feel any different. You might not really believe, but even if you don't believe Jesus will fix it, moving in the right direction requires you to admit your best human effort can't fix it. You might not have the burden lifted, but you will have an open declaration that you acknowledge your fault and desire to move another direction.

The acid test of moral virtue is not where you are on the journey and not even how fast you progress, but only which direction you are moving.

I understand that at the bottom of the pit, you might be running up the down escalator. No matter how hard you run, you may not be able to overcome the machinations that pull you down into the pit, but you are not responsible for the escalator. You are responsible for the running. If you're going to crash, don't crash facing the demons; crash facing the light, or at least trying to face the light.

I'm not asking you to become a saint. I'm asking you to stop looking at the past and turn around. Look the other way. It's absolutely not fair to ignore your guilt. If you can fix what you've done, fix it. If you can't fix what you've done, turn around anyway. It's absolutely not fair that it's Jesus' problem, or God's problem, or anybody's problem other than your own—but removing the burden from yourself is the only way to stop making the problem worse. The only thing more unfair than offloading the responsibility for your faults to Jesus is to keep causing more hurt by refusing to let go of those faults. You can't fix it either way, so stop beating yourself up about it and turn around. Every day that you don't let go, you only become more guilty of magnifying the problem.

So, you're a bad person. You were bad yesterday and bad the day before, and you'll probably be bad tomorrow. Which is worse though, a bad person who is still bad tomorrow because he's facing the demons, or a person who is still bad tomorrow even though he's facing the good? No matter how many bad days lie ahead, only the one facing the light and aiming toward the good will ever overcome the bad.

Failure to leave the past in the past is competitive, not cooperative. If others' pain or pleasure depends on you, you are believing yourself to be the center of their world. This is a lie. You are believing that you are, or should be better than they are. You're not better than they are. Stop trying to figure out who is better and who is worse. Stop thinking you are their judge or they are your judge. Stop thinking you are their victim or they are yours. It's not a competition. You are here to help them and believe it or not, they are here to help you. You have to stop the competition and seek cooperation, even if they don't.

I'm not absolving you of responsibility. This is a practical matter. Today, you don't yet have the strength or resources to recompense all the pain you've caused. If it will ever be possible for you to make amends, it will require you to be further down the path than you are now. When and if you can make amends, do it. Until then, forgive yourself, and keep walking without concerning yourself with how fast you run or who is in front of you.

You don't turn around because you have a guarantee that your hell will get better. You turn around to stop making everyone else's hell worse. Give your problems to God. Give your problems to Jesus. Give the responsibility for your problems to the aether of the universe if that's what it takes. Forgive yourself. Turn toward the good. Face the right direction. Take one step at a time.

Quit Pretending

Can you cooperate with others if you keep lying to them about your depression? Once committed to the truth and then committed to cooperation, you obviously can't keep lying to everyone. You can't keep going through the motions, hiding how you really feel and never say anything.

I understand the nightmare of confronting people and explaining emotions to people who don't understand. Hiding the truth is truly easier, but it's not more helpful. To quit pretending and cooperate means you have to give them some form of true explanation, even if you can't expect them to accept it or understand it.

Sometimes, when I feel the dark thunder clouds gathering, I have to politely explain to others that I feel sick. Even if they can't see the storm coming, you can't commit to the truth if you also pretend it's a sunny day. When the clouds burst and the rain comes, you can pretend you're not all wet, but they will be able to sense something is not right, even if you think you are a good actor. If they don't know why you are wet, you will be blamed for it.

You are depressed. Truth means you stop giving excuses that are untrue, and start giving explanations that are. Yes, they will treat you differently. They might react better. They might react worse. You're committing to quit pretending anyway. You're not committing to make them understand the truth. You cannot control their reaction. You're committing to a chance at cooperation, not a guarantee.

Sometimes, I have to actually explain that "I hate Christmas" even if it does sting a little bit. Sometimes, I have to refuse things I cannot handle. For their sake, and mine, I have to negotiate how much participation in Christmas I can truthfully handle and agree to participate only that much. Maybe I don't say "I hate Christmas" publicly, in those jarring words, but I no longer pretend it's the best day of the year for me just because that's what everyone else wants me to feel. I refuse to do things that would require me to pretend. I agree to do things that others will appreciate without my having to fake it.

I get it. Sometimes you have to pretend or you'll get fired. Sometimes you have to pretend or you'll make things harder. I get it. On the other hand, I found that all that pretending sucks up tons of energy. Pretending should be the exception, not the rule. I quit pretending. When I quit pretending, I also damaged my marriage further, I was judged by others more, and my financial impasse turned into an emergency. Nevertheless, at some point I had to choose between pretending to avoid relationship problems, thus leaving no energy to heal, or trying to get better, even if it hurt those relationships. I didn't have enough energy to pretend and heal at the same time. They will get hurt either way. Isn't it better in the long term to use my energy to address my problem, rather than using my energy to hide from it?

As you know, in the short term, managing the reaction to the truth may require more energy than you have to give, and life may get worse initially. Long term good often requires short term pain. When I admitted my problems to family who I thought should know, they had no idea how to react. When I quit pretending, it made everything worse before it made anything better. They now know the truth, even if they didn't accept or understand it. The truth will only embolden those who see you as a weaker competitor. If they think depression is an excuse, or that it somehow makes you less worthy, let that be their problem. Don't make it your problem by validating the competition. I removed pretending from my long list of things to be depressed about.

Had I not quit pretending, I would never have had enough spare energy to try all of the things I mentioned in the last chapter. Not pretending doesn't mean I said out loud everything the demon screamed at me. It doesn't mean I revealed all the negative feelings and complained to people who didn't understand. It just means I stopped trying to act, and feel, and believe what they wanted me to feel, rather than the truth. I didn't start telling the whole depressing truth, I merely stopped living a depressing lie. Not pretending simply means I quit treating family and friends like competition. If we truly were on the same team, the truth about how far up the mountain I can or cannot climb only helps the team. The quarterback who goes into the game feeling sick, and refuses to tell his teammates he's about to pass out, is competing with his teammates, not cooperating with them.

You've heard the saying, "If you can't say anything nice, don't say anything at all." For me, that means if I have to pretend, I'll say nothing at all rather than lie. Yes, that makes me look grumpy. They see more of my grumbling and negativity in the open. I'm more of a downer to those around me. Yes, it places more burdens and responsibilities on others—but that's the point. I have to remove burdens from myself that are making it worse. Cooperation means I allow them, when they are willing, to shoulder some of the burden —and they can't do that if they don't know what the burdens are.

You don't have to verbalize insults and spew every "true" thought in your head, you just have to stop spewing lies. You can't spare them from the demon. You're not that good of a pretender. No matter how hard you pretend, they will still get hurt. I've heard it said, when the check-engine light comes on, you can actually fix the engine, or you can just unscrew the light bulb. You can pretend the check-engine light is not actually on, but nothing gets fixed that way. Pretending will eventually make it worse. So instead of spending your energy pretending, spend your energy healing, or at least spend your energy for a chance at real cooperation.

To stop pretending means to tell the truth—not the whole truth, the necessary truth:

"I can't handle that right now."
"I need to be alone."
"I know I hurt you. I'm sorry."
"I need help."
"I suffer from depression, and today is not a good day."
"I can't talk about that now, I'll let you know another time."
"Excuse me, I'm about to cry."
"No, I don't feel well. I won't do that."
"I'm sorry, but that's not going to happen."
"I'm about to lose control."

If you pretend you have control, what choice do others have but to blame you for any perceived indiscretion? How is a teammate supposed to treat you when you're not honest? When you admit you are sick, it is true your competitors will use it against you—but that only matters if you join their game. By admitting you are sick to those on your team, you are giving them an excuse to *not* blame you, and maybe even help you.

I'm not suggesting you open your soul to random strangers. I'm suggesting you be honest with those who are close enough to you that they might be able to help. To govern your mind, stop pretending.

Ask for Help

You've most likely been told before that you can't solve depression by yourself. I have a lot of problems with that statement, because it reinforces what a depressed person already feels—that they are fundamentally helpless. Not only that, but so much of the way "they" try and help, is anything but helpful. So much of depression is you trying to compete with others by proving you don't need help, and others trying to compete with you by proving they know better than you. None of this is helpful.

"You can't do it alone" is true, but it's also a lie when out of context. When they don't understand, what they consider "help" can make everything worse. Real help is not what others want to give; it is what you are willing to receive. Only you can make the distinction clear.

At my worst, I quit everything. I quit trying to earn a living, and either my wife had to support the family by herself, or we would … well … whatever comes after foreclosure on the house. I remember constantly ruminating on the hopeless proposition of how we would live without a home, or how I could possibly ask anyone for a floor to sleep on, given my emotional instability. How could I possibly handle the stress of living with someone else who did not understand? It seemed it would be better to abandon my family than to force them through that.

My wife had earned some income independently doing a variety of part-time endeavors, but she had basically been out of the workforce for a while. She did the extremely hard thing of taking it upon herself to become the sole breadwinner in our home. I acknowledge that I forced an unfair choice onto her, but no other help she could have provided would have taken as much weight off my shoulders. By taking that burden on herself, even if somewhat involuntarily, she saved my life.

I survived only in a vicious circle of no money without a job, no job without health, and no health without money. She broke that impasse. By removing the weight of working a job and making it so I didn't have to earn the money, she allowed me to focus on other tiny little itsy bitsy steps up the ladder.

Not everyone has a partner who can do something that big. However, if those who share your life want to cooperate, and you are willing to commit to the truth, you can tell them bluntly what would actually help. They won't understand. In the worst-case scenario, nothing will improve. Best case, though, even though they don't understand, they might do what you need anyway. Without your specific request for help, they won't even have that option.

I cannot count how many things I asked my wife to do that she didn't understand and didn't do. But in the end, she removed the biggest weight—earning a living.

Help doesn't have to be something big like a job or a home. It can be as simple as a doctor helping, or a therapist listening. It doesn't have to be a lifelong commitment. It can be a one-time favor like help with household chores, errands, or eliminating the need to plan an activity or meal. When you constantly fail at so many responsibilities, someone who takes even a small responsibility off your breaking back becomes a lifesaver.

For "help" to actually be helpful and lessen your burdens, you must make clear to others what you would accept and appreciate. For the quarterback and the receiver to cooperate, it makes a big difference if they discuss in advance where the quarterback should run, and where the receiver will be, and when. If you don't talk about it in advance, you'll get something that might be counterproductive. Without a play call, the quarterback can still throw the ball and you can still catch it. It's just that many more of those attempts fail.

To cooperate, you must take the initiative yourself. No matter how much you wish they understood, they don't. Even if they wanted to help, they usually don't see the need. They don't know how to help and they don't know how to ask. Unfortunately, our modern society often frowns on those who ask for help. Societal tradition enforces a culture of pulling your own weight and attaches a stigma to dependency. You have to reject that lie with the others. Don't think of asking for help as humiliating. It's not sad that you have to ask for cooperation; it's sad that they cannot.

You have to tell them exactly how they can help. Only you know which small stepping stone to prioritize on your journey and only you know what "simple" responsibility weighs you down. They might not do it, but to get effective cooperation—to get the help—you have to ask.

To govern the mind, ask for specific help.

This is the first trick to governing your mind: replace competition with cooperation.

15
Triggers

When you feel depressed, you feel out of control. You fail so often and so easily that you start to believe any effort is futile. Remember, though, we have agreed to embrace the truth. As discussed earlier, the truth is that while you can't do everything, you can do something; and while you might not be able to do more, you can do differently!

Accepting that truth and doing differently means governing the mind—the part you can control. First, start looking for cooperation. Second, control your triggers before they control you. While you may not have complete control of your emotions or your demon at the low points of the roller coaster, you can take control of what you think and what you do at the higher points, before that uncontrollable situation arrives. By governing your mind when you can, you can prevent some of the emotional nosedives and better endure those you cannot prevent.

Take Responsibility

Every time a trigger provokes an emotional reaction, your brain rewires itself just a little bit to make that reaction a little bit easier the next time. If you don't take back control from the triggers, they will never give control back to you.

That you cannot control your reaction to an unpredictable trigger may be true. Once your brain rewires itself to react, you may not be able to control the *reaction*—but you can control the *trigger*. I'm not claiming you have complete control over triggers, but you do have *some* control. No matter what seeds you plant in your garden, you can't avoid the unknown weeds that you don't plant. You can, however, pull out a few of the weeds while they are small, before they take over. You can avoid planting seeds you know are nasty and diseased. Even if you can't undo the triggers *after the fact*, that doesn't mean you have no control *beforehand*. You have to reshape your habits and revamp your surroundings *before* a trigger has the opportunity to upset the delicate emotional balance. Accept responsibility for what you can control.

My most ingrained trigger was household clutter. A tissue that didn't make it into the garbage could send my emotions raging out of control. It began a cascade of demonic logic. If the tissue brought the depression that I hated, I started hating the person that left out the tissue.

> *They are so awful. I've asked them to pick up their trash and they essentially spit in my face.*

My shoulder demon, unprompted, would remind me of every offense this "hateful" person had ever committed. Of course, rationally, I knew a tissue outside the garbage did not prove anything about a person's motives, so I felt guilty for such judgmental feelings.

> *I must be awful. I must be hateful. I must be worthless.*

You already know how the abyss of rumination's faulty logic gets much worse, so I'll stop.

Tissues, food that was not put away, dishes not washed, laundry not folded, beds not made, bathrooms not cleaned—the list of my triggers was never-ending, and it was always someone else's fault—my wife's fault for making the mess, leaving the mess, not teaching the kids to clean, or not respecting my request to keep my space clutter-free.

I knew many of those thoughts were just plain wrong, logically; but that's not how triggers work. They trigger you whether it makes sense or not. Of course, rationally, I knew my wife couldn't do it all. She can't do everything, but I couldn't do anything. I refused to earn the money, I refused to be the dad. I refused to cook the meals. I refused to clean the house. Only someone who has experienced that hellhole can understand that I really couldn't do those things.

My wife didn't know it, but when she got a full time job and became the family's sole provider, she changed both our lives. Because she took the responsibility of earning a living off my back, it freed up just enough energy for me to consider the next step that I could take. I couldn't work. I couldn't be a good father. I couldn't go to church, or fix my stupid body, but maybe … just maybe … I could clean the bathroom. If I cleaned the bathroom, it might stop me from reacting poorly when my wife didn't clean the bathroom.

After all, I did know how to clean the bathroom. Before the darkest days, I was a partner in the household, like a normal person. You'd think 20 minutes a week cleaning the bathroom wouldn't be a big deal. You might think that—if you've never been overwhelmed with depression. Fortunately, because I had started collagen, and because my wife removed the burden of earning the money, I had just enough energy to seriously consider not only cleaning the bathroom, but taking on the responsibility of all the household cleaning. *Should I make it my job to clean the house?*

Before you can do anything to help, you have to accept responsibility for your triggers. The responsibility has to be yours, because "they don't understand!" You can't expect them to be responsible for preventing your reactions when they don't understand. No matter how many times you ask them to change or how many times you try to explain your emotions to them, from their perspective, it's just a tissue—or whatever it is for you. To them, it's not a trigger. They don't understand that to you it is an invitation to hell. Since they don't understand, and your reaction—voluntary or not—is *your* reaction, you have to be responsible for it.

Let me reemphasize that I considered taking on all the household cleaning responsibility only after years of smaller stepping stones, not as the first step. I agonized over that decision for months because, as you know, if I took on such a big responsibility and failed, I feared it would send me back into the depths of hell.

Eliminate Triggers

Finally, I told my wife I did not expect her to clean the bathroom, or do the dishes, or mop the floors any more. The sole responsibility for cleaning had to be mine so that I had no justification to blame her. I had to eliminate the trigger! Even if the garbage was technically her fault, my reaction to it was not her responsibility. If the house were clean, I wouldn't have nearly as many dirty tissues and unwiped countertops to feed the demon. Every crumpled tissue I threw away, every crumb I swept, and every sink, countertop, or floor I cleaned on my best day would be one less provocation to worry about on my worst.

I couldn't be triggered by something that wasn't there, and if it were there, and I had already promised to make it my responsibility and not hers, I certainly couldn't blame her for my emotional crash. Sometimes, I don't have the energy to clean, and the bathroom is still disgusting, but it's much easier to accept my own excuse than hers. I can no longer rationalize a way to make her the cause of my cascade into hell.

Nothing actually changed about my depression, my weaknesses, or my reactions. The only thing that changed was my decision to be responsible for it. I governed those thoughts that said I had no control. I set aside the thoughts that said I could not control the reaction and concentrated on what I could control—the triggers. Yes, I had to clean more, and that was a huge undertaking given my exhausted state, but all that really changed was my mind.

Once I actually accepted the responsibility, the freedom from the freak show of trigger-happy demons in my home saved more than enough energy to allow me to handle my new obligations. I've now been solely responsible for the cleaning in my house for about five years. Despite my fear of failure, making that commitment did more to change my emotional stability on the inside than any other mental effort. By eliminating the trigger, I freed myself of an unbearable weight. Without that weight, my mind could consider the next small step—and the next.

You know that booger that sends you off the deep end? You know that tissue that you can't control? Take control of the thing before it takes control of you. Make a plan to change your environment, avoid that location, or hide the trigger. Avoid it, shield it, or destroy it.

To govern your mind, eliminate your triggers.

Create Habits

Depression has been rewiring your brain and eliminating any sense of reward. The neurochemical processes in your brain have been trained by demons to believe lies. Every time you prevent the demon from reinforcing those lies, you start the process of restoring the proper circuits. Your dopamine, serotonin, oxytocin, adrenaline, and endorphins have all been responding weakly or incorrectly.

The circuits may never be restored 100 percent, but the habits that stop the haywire can. Every time you succeed at preventing a trigger, every time you take a tiny responsibility and don't fail, every time you spare an argument, feel the tiniest relief, or see a glimmer of hope, you move that circuit one step further from disrepair and one step closer to health.

You're right, you cannot necessarily control your reactions, your emotions, or the circumstances that have sent you off the cliff. Once the circumstances of your life, the frailty of the body, and deceptions of the demons have manipulated you into bad habits, you are not in control. Very, very, true, despite what they don't understand. You can, however, create new habits—different habits.

Why habits? Because ignoring one trigger one time won't work. You have to do it over, and over, and over. It has to become a habit. Knowing the psychology of forming habits, I insisted that my wife was not even allowed to do the dishes anymore. I had to force myself to do it with no escape routes. Only if I forced myself to do it every day would it become a habit, and only if it became a habit, would it gradually rewire my emotional circuits.

For the first few months I hated every minute of it. Today, I don't even think about asking my wife to clean the bathroom or do the dishes. It's not hard anymore, because it's a habit. I cannot begin to explain how that single decision changed our marriage. I cannot begin to describe how many triggers that single decision has spared. I cannot begin to communicate how much less pain I now suffer. You can only know by your own experience.

I know how hard it is to believe that you can change anything, or that it will work. I know how impossible it sounds to find the energy. I know that you may not understand how it will take the guilt, or the pain, or the loneliness away. You can't accept it just because I say so. I beg you to take that leap of faith for yourself. Govern your own thoughts and decide for yourself to take on the responsibility of eliminating one of your own triggers. Then, repeat it often enough, and endure long enough, that it becomes a habit.

To govern your mind, you must create new habits.

Governing the mind doesn't mean you have to feel guilty for bad emotional reactions. You don't have to govern what you can't control. Governing the mind means controlling what you can control—triggers. Stop trying to control the reactions after the fact; start controlling the habits beforehand.

16
Lies

Governing the mind means seeking cooperation, eliminating triggers, and lastly, overcoming deceptive lies.

Depression Increasing

Before I talk about lies, I should point out that for a lot of people in the world, life just keeps getting better. Global extreme poverty is falling, access to clean water increasing, infant mortality plummeting, worldwide literacy increasing, pollution improving, and so on.

Depression isn't one of those things that is improving. According to the Substance Abuse and Mental Health Services Administration, 22.5 million adults in the US experienced a major depressive episode in 2022. Another 4.8 million adolescents experienced major depression. That's over 27 million people! About 17 million of those reported serious suicidal thoughts.[1] The true number of people affected by the demon is much higher. Depression has been increasing for decades. How many more people suffer with no diagnosis, no understanding, or were not willing to answer the survey honestly? How many more have mild symptoms?

Divorce rates remain stubbornly high. Obesity is increasing. Opioid addiction has been worsening. Debt is worsening. Wage growth has stagnated. Jobs are being automated and outsourced out of existence. Political division has become a source of constant stress in the culture, and even among close friends and family. Pandemics, inflation, war—there is no end to the list of stressors.

I believe the stress of the cultural divide in our modern world will only continue to make depression more common. I believe more and more people will find themselves in life circumstances in which they question their own self-worth, their faith, and their significance in the world at large. My religious faith informs me that a satanic force deliberately seeks to divide us and create antagonism and misery in the end times. I believe in a literal evil that seeks to make you and me miserable. Even if you don't believe in the devil, purely objective measurements show depression is increasing.

Despite the fact that millions of people suffer depression, each one of us feels completely alone. What irony. I know you understand. Either you have no contact with those other depressed people, they are not honest about their feelings in public, or they have isolated themselves. Somehow, we are all alone, together. Their depression differs from yours. They might understand something, but they still don't understand you, not exactly.

While it may feel lonely on the inside, you know objectively that countless others suffer. Whether it is diet, environmental pollution, or metaphysical evil—or who knows what else—something about our reality drags more and more people into depression's pit.

Deception Increasing

In addition to whatever material causes may be physically increasing depression, one cause is certain. Forces of evil are at war with your mind. Power-hungry, self-serving narcissists want to manipulate and deceive you for their own gain. Whether by their own schemes or by the instigation of some transcendent evil doesn't matter. Real power players are trying to deceive you into believing lies and adopting paradigms of thinking that will ensure their own control and pleasure at the expense of yours. The political gatekeepers, government propagandists, and corporate marketers keep getting better and better at lying to you. It gets harder and harder to know who to trust and what is really true. The more lies we believe as a society the harder it will be to avoid depression's sticky tentacles.

Good men and women don't want to believe it, but these powerful interests actually conduct scientific testing to learn how to manipulate your beliefs without your knowledge. The corpus of research has been growing for decades, and studying it has been one of my favorite pastimes.

Deceptions and depression go hand in hand, which should come as no surprise to Bible-believers. Deception presents as one of the hallmark signs of the end times, as shown here in 2 Timothy 3.

> "Know also, that in the last days perilous times shall come … evil men and seducers shall wax worse and worse, deceiving and being deceived."

Depression causes more and more people to believe lies. Believing more lies causes more and more people to become depressed. Whatever the cause of the great deception and the great depression of our times, you have a unique seat at the table.

Whether they are lies you tell yourself or lies others use to manipulate you, how do you recognize the deception?

Counseling & Therapy

What about counseling? Is therapy part of the problem or part of the solution? Isn't most behavioral therapy based on recognizing misguided thoughts and correcting self-deception? I say you should adopt an attitude of cooperation and forgiveness rather than competition, so you can tell the truth, quit pretending, and ask for help. Work through your thought processes to head off the demons, take responsibility, and prevent triggers. This all sounds like what psychologists do. Does that mean I recommend counseling?

Various different therapies have been shown in research studies to help depression as well or better than drugs. Talking to a psychologist or therapist, who has been trained to help you work through your thoughts, can definitely help. They can help you develop habits to manage your weaker inclinations and strive for more stability.

While I am not a licensed psychologist, the study of psychology has been a lifelong pursuit of mine. I have dedicated myself especially to the psychology of persuasion, deception, and motivation. Counseling has never been the focus of my interests, but I have learned much about counseling techniques and the scientific basis for them.

I did not personally seek counseling for my depression. Feel free to fault me for that if you wish. Firstly, I knew my problems stemmed primarily from a physical cause, not a psychological one.

Secondly, I could not bring myself to submit to an industry about which I knew so much and disagreed with so vehemently. As a whole, I see the industry of counseling and therapy following cultural whims more than they follow actual science. After spending decades studying deception and manipulation, I find that most therapists and counselors, while well-meaning, fall for the same deceptions and lies that have caused our cultural decay to begin with.

Counselors, on the surface, try to help you identify the incongruities in your own thoughts and the logical fallacies of your own beliefs. I support that. The pursuit of truth is basically my life's mission statement.

Strangely, that's why I'm often skeptical of counseling. Generally, we don't have false beliefs and inconsistent logic in spite of cultural influence, but specifically because of it. The "normal" life that counselors try to help you live is far from the ideal of truth. The "normal" most the world aspires to is the very deceptive, manipulative society that contributed to your problems in the first place.

The stated goal of most counseling is to help you cope with, and develop more effective behaviors to succeed and grow within your community. That goal fundamentally contradicts my core principles. I do not want to conform to a society and culture whose deceptions and manipulations make my life harder. I only want to conform to the truth—to reality—even if that reality proves harder than conformity—even if the truth means I must fight against societal norms. Proven therapies can help depressed people feel better, but I believe it too often comes at the expense of the truth. By learning to conform better to society and its deceptions, a depressed person often learns to feel better only because they fit in better and conform better. I believe you cannot conform to society without also conforming to societal deceptions—which in the long term will only create more misery.

I am not suggesting you don't talk to a professional. I trust neither medical doctors nor mental health professionals as a group. I judge only individuals, not groups. Individual counselors can be helpful and amazing, as long as their goal is truth and cooperation, rather than ego and conformity. If you know a good therapist who fits the bill and helps, counseling is undoubtedly one of the steps and resources you can take on your path.

To trust a counselor, you have to know how to recognize the lies that they don't even know they are promoting. If you choose to seek counseling, avoid the following dangerous lies:

- It's simple.
- You are a victim.
- Trust in the process.
- Put yourself first.
- It's not your job.
- Do what feels good.
- Avoid what feels bad.
- Try to fit in.

Explaining what I mean by these deceptions and many others is beyond the scope of this book. As I mentioned, understanding influence, persuasion, and deception has been a lifelong pursuit of mine. As I started to recover gradually from my darkest years, I began developing a program and writing about "12 Lies that Make Your Life Harder." As I watched the culture blossom into chaos over the last few years, I felt compelled to take a break from that project and write this book first. I know that the lies I see promulgated continuously before us are dragging many others into the pit of depression, and having been there, I felt compelled to articulate my experience before I offered any advice about recognizing the lies.

Any counselor who can help me recognize the lies I unwittingly believe is on my team. If you want to know more about the "12 lies"—those subtle deceptions that pervade every facet of modern life—visit my website at MichaelDGriffith.com.

All of the lies can be encapsulated in the competitive worldview we have already discussed. Question the advice of anyone who wants you to act a certain way because others think they are better than you, because others have placed limits on you, or because you must climb the ladder of success to a position of higher virtue, higher understanding, or higher achievement, than those who are not like you.

Most therapists have not experienced severe depression for themselves. I know it would be unreasonable to say you can only get help from someone who has truly been there themself, but unlike most of the "they" that don't understand, professional counselors are particularly dangerous. These professionals have talked to enough depressed people to learn the right words to say that gain your confidence, even if they truly don't understand at all—or worse, even if they do not actually have your best interests at heart. Often, if they have not experienced severe depression, they see themselves higher on that competitive ladder—more virtuous than you, proud that they, as professionals, can help those lowly depressed people. They will hide that elitism inside, but if it ever reveals itself peeking out, run away. Real therapy is a cooperation among the weak, not a competition to prove who is right, who is virtuous, or who is strong.

Speak Words

Good therapy works through conversation—speaking. You have to speak. Fortunately, you can speak for yourself with or without paying a therapist.

In depression, thoughts, emotions, and reasoning get all tied up in knots. We feel hopeless in the midst of those ruminations. No matter how confusing it feels, never let a counselor, therapist, or anyone else explain it for you. A good counselor will always let you say it in your own words, not theirs. It's cliché, but true. Most of what a good counselor does is listen to you, and help you talk through your own thoughts. A counselor who spends the time talking, teaching, and advice giving rather than letting you work it out yourself is a huge red flag.

One simple principle in life applies to almost all people, depressed or not: you don't actually know a thing if you can't explain it. You may attribute this thought to any number of various sources.

In that vicious circle of rumination, you find great difficulty differentiating between reason and emotion. You have to somehow sort out which ruminations are grounded in reality and which ruminations are actually irrational emotion. It's very easy to let someone else, like a psychologist, explain it for you in simple words that sound good. When it sounds good, it's really easy to trust their advice—even when it's bad advice. Don't accept other people's words, including mine. Speak your own words.

Words can solve the problem of deception. Words have power! We all know the possible clarity that can come from "talking out your problem" with friends and therapists because as you talk it out, you understand it better. To explain your thoughts to someone else, you have to first make sure you know what you believe yourself. That happens in the very act of speaking.

In the rumination of depression, you fake it. You can feel like you've come to a conclusion or come to an impasse, when you never actually explained it to anyone. Rumination can feel like articulating words and sound reasoning, even when it's not. You can ponder the hopelessness of your life, but if you never actually communicate it in words to someone else, you can never prove to yourself which part comes from valid reasoning and which from pure emotion. It doesn't even really matter who you talk to—a friend, a parent, a therapist—as long as you address your words to someone other than yourself. When you talk to yourself, you take shortcuts and leave words out. When explaining something to yourself gets hard, you jump ahead, assuming you already know what you mean. You don't! You can only prove to yourself that you know what you really think and believe when you take the time to actually put it into your own words, without shortcuts.

No matter how alone you feel, speaking words always remains an option. Even if you have no one who will listen, you can get out a piece of paper and expound your thoughts to an imaginary reader. Scientific studies have shown incredible effectiveness at improving feelings just by putting them on paper—in words. Writing works even better than speaking, because it's permanent. The permanence of written words forces you to articulate your thoughts even more accurately.

Why does speaking work? Because first it lets you unburden yourself, and in a sense, disassociate from it. Second, speaking or writing forces you to use the rational part of your brain. Forming a sentence happens in a completely different part of your brain than the part that imposes emotions. That's why putting emotions into words is so hard. Third, once you actually do put it into words and prove to yourself how you feel and what you know, you start to see new connections and perspectives. Fourth, rumination never ends, but words must end. You can struggle for hours finding the right words, but once you say the right words, you know you are done. When you are overwhelmed with emotion, you don't have words. Not surprising then, when you do put it into words, you no longer have the same emotions.

This book is a perfect example. I have tried to put into words what depression feels like. If reading my words resonates at all with how you feel, you have probably noticed that it alleviates a little bit of the weight. Just knowing that someone can articulate it, lessens the burden. The effect grows by orders of magnitude more powerful when you use your own words. When you speak or write your own feelings, and you find the right words, and articulate a course of action, you will experience an otherwise impossible emotion. It feels right!

How often when suffering from depression does anything "feel right?" By articulating your thoughts, even bad thoughts, you can feel right about how you explain it. I have volumes of my personal feelings written in my journals, many of which I hope no one will ever see. I didn't write them to be read. I wrote them to be sane.

Put your feelings and plans into words. Tell a friend. Tell a therapist. Tell a lover. Tell a diary. Don't ruminate on emotions disguised as thoughts.

Put it into words!

When you speak, you force yourself to govern your thoughts. If they truly are your own thoughts, and not taken from someone else as a shortcut, you can more easily avoid the lies of the world at large that contribute to your depression. Every one of those deceptions that your words expose starves one of depression's demons. Committing to the truth and governing your mind means controlling your words.

Govern the mind. Seek cooperation. Eliminate triggers. Speak truth and expose lies.

---

[1] "Key Substance Use and Mental Health Indicators in the United States: Results from the 2022 National Survey on Drug Use and Health," https://www.samhsa.gov/data/sites/default/files/reports/rpt42731/2022-nsduh-nnr.pdf

Part V: Yield to the Spirit

17
Meaning

I believe the rest of this book is the most important part. What I am about to say is, in fact, the whole reason I wrote this book to begin with.

How do you find meaning in the pain? Yield to the spirit!

No matter what the cause of your depression, body or mind—or both—identifying the cause and taking baby steps is not enough. You need more than a reason not to die; you need a reason to live. Life needs meaning. This section of the book, part five, gives a unique perspective on finding meaning in the suffering. Meaning does not guarantee health or lack of health. Meaning justifies the health or lack of health.

Religion

"Meaning" is one step beyond the psychological. It's more theological than biological. Meaning stems from your worldview of the higher powers that govern the universe and your soul, whatever god or physical principle you believe that authority to be. Whatever physical or metaphysical force connects you to the universe at large, you must yield to that spirit.

I am not preaching the dogma of any specific religion. I am sharing the changes in my own beliefs that allowed me to cope with my pain. Please do not ascribe the opinions I share to any religion or denomination; they are mine alone.

I don't believe I could have been more honest, more devoted, or more believing in my faith. Nevertheless, when the most faithful in my religion proved they didn't understand my experience, when the promises they preached were absent from my life, when God didn't answer my prayers, and my experience contradicted my faith, I had to abandon my religion. I could no longer pretend to agree, no matter how much I once believed.

It took me years to sort through what I personally believed versus what a church taught. To find meaningful faith, I began to consider everything from atheism to mysticism. I rejected some of my family's faith and accepted some truths that they would deny. I seek only the truth, and that pursuit will never end. What I believe now about the meaning of suffering does not align exactly with mainstream Christianity nor any single religion of which I am aware.

Whether you call it theology, or religion, or soul searching—in the bubble of depression you need a way to make sense of the suffering. Finding that truth—that meaning—in my life's pains and failures made a bigger difference than any other step on the road to recovery.

This may be the most controversial chapter I write, but I consider it the most important. I suspect that religious readers who are committed to a specific dogma, without having experienced the contradictions of deep depression, will dispute much of what I say. If you want to argue with my theology, then you don't understand my point. If what you already believe isn't working and you're still miserable, isn't it worth considering that what you believe might be part of the problem? Or at least incomplete?

If my perspective adds meaning to your experience, thank God. If not, I choose not to argue about it. Trying to argue away each other's spiritual scaffolding won't help either of us. Those who have wallowed around in the abyss of hell would never try to deny that meaning to someone else in that pain. I wish you the best at finding meaning for yourself, so please consider the following perspective with an open mind.

The Afterlife

Atheists, who reject God altogether, must see good and evil in terms of chance, with no supernatural cause. Your problems are the effect of some material cause, or they stem from a genetic lottery. Your ticket came up short. Life requires no ultimate purpose or meaning. You just have to make the most of the hand you were dealt. Whether you live or die has no existential meaning. If you die, you simply cease to exist.

Some secularists say their atheism encourages them to live life to the fullest. Pop culture makes atheism out to be a greater incentive to stay alive, since it's your only chance. In depression, though, you may feel you have exhausted your scientific options. I submit that basing life on materialism, when you have no material hope of a better life, doesn't make you feel any better.

Those people who think their material worldview is a better incentive to stay alive, have never been depressed enough to understand the feeling of not having any material hope.

> *If there is nothing I can do about it ... and it doesn't matter anyway ... why shouldn't I take my own life?*

I remember many times thinking to myself that if I knew there were no afterlife—nothing after death—I would gladly cease to exist rather than endure the torment of my personal hell on earth. In my deep depression, believing in atheism would make it easier to die, not harder. Atheism provided me no meaning in suffering. Extinguishing your consciousness might offer hope of relief, but it doesn't offer meaning. Materialism in depression provided me a reason to die, not a reason to live.

If you do believe that consciousness ceases after this life, you must at least consider the alternative. What if you're wrong? What if you end the body, only to discover that consciousness endures? In that case, death may not solve anything!

Most religions, Christians included, believe in an enduring consciousness of some form. Some believe that if you are not "saved" while in a mortal body, you immediately move from the psychological hell of depression into the literal hellfire of eternal damnation. In this case, the last resort is no resort at all—just a change of venue.

Others believe your eternal reward or punishment depends on your obedience to the rules. They usually consider suicide as one of the worst rules you can break, and even if they believe in eventual salvation, they believe you must be punished for taking a life. The punishment looks a lot like the hell of depression, and so death still doesn't solve the problem.

I find no meaning and no sense of peace, justice, or divinity in being forced to endure psychological hell as some sort of a test. They say God tests me, apparently to see whether I will submit to an invisible slave master in heaven without any option of escape, even after death. I must worship the very being who created me in hell against my will. I either suffer voluntarily or involuntarily. I have no further choice. If I somehow pick the right religion and pass a test—with no instructions—I escape the pain in the afterlife. Otherwise, I'm eternally damned. I find no meaning in such theologies.

Other countless belief systems teach that after death my soul releases back into the cosmos, or becomes recycled in some way to become part of another life, or another iteration of experience. That's nice, I guess, but my pain right now is wholly individual to me. No other earthly being truly understands. If I believed in any version of mysticism, it might offer hope in the sense that the pain could end, but the prospect of releasing my individuality into the aether offers no meaning in the suffering of the here and now. Don't tell me about karma. I cannot accept that I deserve my pain without knowing what I did wrong or without a chance to make amends. That's not just. That's not divine.

Finding meaning, as I describe it, doesn't mean I hope for a hypothetical, peaceful reward in eternity. I don't need answers later. I need enough understanding right now to endure right now. If my suffering doesn't go away, I can only endure by making peace with it now.

Theodicy

In every worldview, believers hope for something better in the hereafter to explain and compensate for the apparent injustice of the here and now. If you accept any ethical or moral framework to life, the reality of both good and evil is self-evident. *Bad things happen to good people. Life is unfair.* I don't see how anyone in the pit of despair can feel differently when they look out into the world and see that others do not have to suffer as they do.

When philosophers and theologians explain the problem of evil in spite of a "good" God, they call it theodicy. Every religion has its own theodicy.

- God is not actually all-powerful.
- God is not actually good.
- Pain is not actually bad.
- What we perceive as evil is part of a plan.
- Evil is the absence of good.
- Life is a test.
- Life is a simulation.
- Evil is from man's free will, not God.
- God does not exist at all.

I won't delve into the theological discussions of each point, other than to point out that none of them provides meaning to someone in the depths of depression.

I personally find no comfort in any of these theodicies. In every case, the creator—whether it be the vibrations of the cosmos or a literal god—created my soul and body out of nothing. He/She/It forces me to live a life in this evil, unjust world, and I have no say in the matter. Their doctrines admit to evil here and now, excusing it away with the hope of a hypothetical future eternity in which God will compensate us for all the injustice. Unfortunately, they all disagree on what we have to do to obtain that hypothetical future peace.

I have come to believe another theodicy—one that fundamentalists of almost all religious persuasions roundly dismiss and ignore. Most theologians have never even considered it. Other theologians reject it out of hand—not because it doesn't make sense, but because accepting it would require them to rethink too many of their dogmatic, unquestioned beliefs.

If you have suffered what I think you've suffered, then you have probably rejected such dogmatic assumptions already. You've been questioning yourself and your beliefs for a long time. I trust you will listen with a more open mind.

Consent

The answer is consent. I don't mean that bad things happen to good people because of free will in this life. I mean that before you were born, you consented to the life you have now. You chose the pain. You chose the despair. You chose the hell.

Never! ... That does not bring me peace! I would never choose this!

Please let me elaborate.

In our society, we consider rape to be a grave sin and evil. Yet the exact same physical act, with consent of all involved, we consider to be the highest good. Why?

In our society, we consider murder to be satanic. Why, then, does the overwhelming majority believe that assisted suicide in old age or terminal disease shows compassion and should be legal?

Likewise, to forcibly impale another person's most sensitive body parts, such as nipples or genitalia, is considered torture. Why, then, do we consider a body piercer to be an acceptable profession?

Consent changes everything.

I happened to be raised in a branch of Christianity that teaches that our souls existed before this life and that we had a choice to participate. My upbringing made the following argument easier for me to accept, but it may be new to you. I am not preaching a church doctrine. My upbringing taught me to believe in an eternal premortal consciousness, but beyond that, I was not taught in church what I'm about to say.

I have come to believe that before this life, I was shown exactly what lives I could live, exactly what significant choices I could be faced with, and the outcomes that would result from each choice. I was shown the pain. I was shown depression. I was shown exactly how I might abandon my responsibilities and hurt others. I was shown exactly what could have been and exactly what could not be —and I agreed.

What is evil, unjust, and pernicious when inflicted on you against your will takes on a whole new meaning when experienced with your consent.

It would not be just for God to create me and force me to live a life in pain without my consent. It wouldn't even be just for God to create me and force me to live a life of pleasure without my consent. I see no logical way around the premise. If God exists and God is just, I had to consent, or God wouldn't be just, and God wouldn't exist.

You may initially reject this concept. *No way! Impossible! I would never choose this!* I understand. I have uttered those words to myself countless times. *I would never consent to this!*

But what if you did?

What if you not only agreed to your life, but what if you handpicked your exact challenges, on purpose? Would that make a difference in the justice or injustice of your suffering? I'm not asking you to necessarily accept or deny my beliefs. I'm just asking you to consider if it would provide more "meaning" to your situation.

Why would you choose such pain?

Why does a teenager want to taste a beer when he or she will almost certainly not enjoy it the first time?

Why does anyone smoke their first cigarette when she expects it to make her vomit?

Why do fighters enter the ring knowing they will leave with their nose broken, bloodied, and in pain for days?

Why do kids play sports where they will be tackled, shot with BBs, or stung with paintballs?

Why do police officers and military recruits volunteer to go to war?

Why do we watch horror movies that intentionally provoke fear?

Why do we watch dramas that intentionally provoke tears?

Why do we let the doctor amputate a leg when it's diseased?

Why do we prick the infant's heel and incite heart-wrenching screams just to take a blood sample?

Why has every child run barefoot in the snow when they know it's cold?

Why has every child touched the flame when they know it will burn?

Why have you taken a job that you don't want?

Why have you denied yourself pleasure and saved money for later?

Why do we practice musical instruments until our fingers bleed and practice swinging at pitches that are so fast we know we will miss?

Why do you exercise or lift weights when it hurts?

Why do you stay in bad relationships?

Have you ever done something you knew was going to cause a problem just to see what it felt like?

Why? Because we know that when it's over we will understand something that we couldn't have learned any other way. We really do believe that something on the other side of the pain will be worth it. We accept voluntary suffering every day of our lives. Why, then, is it so hard to accept that maybe we did the same thing before this life?

If you consider yourself Christian, the implications of premortal choice may have lots of uncomfortable theological implications, but it doesn't fundamentally change the doctrine that you must submit to Christ to be saved. Nor does the reality of a premortal choice fundamentally alter the core beliefs of any other religion I know.

Consent does, however, provide "meaning." You do not suffer life in depression's abyss because of a vindictive God, because you necessarily committed some great evil, or because of mere happenstance. You experience the pains of your exact challenges because, before the suffering, you agreed that that exact suffering would be worth it for your own personal growth. I am not saying you understood all the vicissitudes of life in every particular. I do claim, however, that you agreed to the circumstances and choices with which you would be faced. At worst, you agreed to your pain. At best, you designed it.

Peace

If true, the ramifications of this theodicy are much more profound than it first appears. However, before I expound on the ramifications, let me explain why I believe it. I don't believe this theology because I learned it in church. I didn't! I don't believe this idea because I read it explicitly in scripture. I didn't! I don't believe this theory because I have more scientific evidence than you do. I don't!

I have only an overwhelming peace and clarity about a subject that used to torment me. I believe I gave my consent to my suffering for one simple reason. When the idea came to me, I was overcome with a sense of peace—a sense of meaning that explained how I could choose the unthinkable and how it would work out for good.

I never abandoned God. In my journey, I tried to find the truth with Him, and I tried to find the truth without Him. I tried to find truth in deism, theism, and atheism. In the end, despite the fact that I still do not have a monopoly on truth, I could not find peace in an existence devoid of deity.

I cannot reconcile every doctrine of my religion with my real experience. Nevertheless, I believe in scripture. I believe in God. I believe in Christ, and I believe in divine inspiration, or what Christians might call the Holy Spirit—that He can "speak peace" (Ps 5:8) to my soul.

I sought that peace for over 20 years, and then one day, all of a sudden, it came. I prayed as I had done countless times before, pleading with God to take the pain away, to explain the purpose of it all, and to somehow make me understand. Perhaps by accident or perhaps by divine inspiration, I asked, "God, did I choose this life, on purpose?" In answer to that prayer, my mind diverted down the rabbit hole, pursuing a train of thought I had never before considered.

The ramifications of this theodicy terrify me because I understand why someone would take their own life. I understand why and how I would want my consciousness to end. However, if before my birth I purposely chose to intentionally experience a life in that depression, then choosing to end that life not only hurts those I leave behind, but it actually thwarts the very plan I created for myself, and denies me the one experience and lesson I previously knew that I needed. If I accept that I chose this challenge from a more enlightened perspective, then no matter how much it makes sense to end my life, I must believe that in the eternal scheme of things, doing so would only set back my own self-directed progress.

Yes, this theodicy gives me meaning, but it also makes it far more difficult for me to justify my own suicide. Therefore, I now truly believe that taking my one life is wrong, not because it's some unpardonable mortal sin, but because doing so would primarily be working against myself—against my own eternal desires. Yielding to the spirit means submitting willingly to the life that your soul, your eternal spirit, has lovingly selected for you.

How does this help me live with depression?

Let me explain the missing piece of the puzzle that restored my faith and restored meaning to my life.

18
Sacrifice

How does the theodicy of consent bring meaning to the pit? Consent explains how a just god could inflict what seems unjust. However, that understanding alone didn't satisfy me. My consent does not make my life better or easier. Consent does not take away the guilt for all the negativity and hurt I've caused in this world. Consent doesn't bring meaning to the hell I've forced others to endure with me.

Or does it?

If my theodicy of consent is true, God had to keep this premortal choice hidden from us. Think what would happen if people actually believed this. You can never share what I'm about to say with those you love or who love you. Just as God didn't tell you, you can never tell anyone else. The next few paragraphs may help you. They may bring meaning to your experience, but "they"—the others in your life—will take offense.

That day when I offered that prayer and asked, "God, did I choose this life, on purpose?" I was overcome with peace. Not just because the answer was yes, but because the implication and ramifications of that affirmative answer sent my thoughts spiraling into a new world of understanding.

If you accept that you agreed to your life's challenges in advance, or perhaps even designed your life's challenges, then logically you must draw another conclusion, which, in that moment of prayer, came to me with sudden clarity. That is—if you agreed to your life, then "they" agreed to theirs. If you agreed to life in depression's hellhole, then by agreeing to share your life, others agreed to share your hell. They agreed to all those awful things they knew you would do to ruin their lives.

What if you didn't just consent to your life, but actually planned it? If you planned your life, then they planned theirs! In that case, not only did they agree to the pain you have caused them, but perhaps they specifically asked for it. They designed their lives as much as you designed yours. It had to be a mutual undertaking. You are not in your life by accident. You designed a life with challenges that you personally chose to endure for your own eternal benefit. Likewise, before this life, those around you asked you to be part of their life, not in spite of the pain you would cause, but specifically because they knew your hell would provide them an experience they desperately wanted—or more likely needed—for themselves.

You know that pain, and suffering, and injustice, and hell in life? You asked for it! Do you see why God can't say it directly and neither can you! "You asked for it!" How will that go over next time someone you love accuses you of hurting them?

Consider the ramifications of intentional sacrifice. It's likely that some of those people with the greatest challenges in life are actually the most noble souls. Perhaps those who suffer fates worse than depression—disability, abuse, or slavery—actually chose the ultimate sacrifice to live a life not for their own pleasure, but in a manner that would benefit someone they love.

Imagine if someone really wanted and needed to experience the responsibility of taking care of another with a mental or physical disability. For someone to have that experience as a caregiver, another soul must have voluntarily agreed to be the disabled one who receives the care. It's possible that some people whom we consider to be the most unfortunate souls of all humanity are such only because they agreed to suffer for the benefit and at the request of someone else.

I do not justify evil. I'm not excusing violence or condoning hurting others. Some people endure absolutely horrendous experiences. I do not claim to know why anyone would agree to such things, nor can I tell them I believe they did—but I do believe it. I don't look at a horrible victim and think, "Wow! They asked for it! How stupid!" I look at someone who suffers and think, "Wow! They asked for it? What an incredible soul to agree to such an impossibly hard thing!"

In case you haven't made the connection yet, let me spell out the implication for you. Yes, we all suffer the natural consequences of our individual bad choices, but on a broader scale, you might not suffer with such an incredibly hard life because just you are bad. Maybe you accepted such an incredibly hard sacrifice because you are trying to be good!

Responsibility

Does this mean you have an excuse to be mean, or lazy, or cause pain to others? No, and unfortunately, if the Bible actually said directly that "you asked for it," people would use it as an excuse to act badly.

While you should not use this knowledge as an excuse to slack off, you can use it as a justification to forgive yourself for all of those times you did cause pain, **unintentionally**—when it was out of your control, for which you cannot compensate others. Those **unintentional** offenses were meant to be—and will actually be appreciated in the hereafter by those who agreed to them.

In the eternal scheme of things, you and they agreed to the circumstances of life for a good reason. You might not remember exactly what that reason is, but there is a reason! There is a purpose! There is meaning in your suffering! Not only is there a reason, but it's a reason you would understand and accept if you could remember it.

I can only guess at how my being an unintentionally awful person so many times made a net positive difference in the lives of my family. How can it be a good thing? I will never know until I reach the afterlife, but I can guess. My depression forced my wife to be independent on a scale she never planned—to get additional education, a new career, and new friends who would support her when I would not. She hated it. Today, on the other end of that challenge, she exhibits no fondness for the memory of what she calls the "dark years," but I don't think she would say she regrets those hard choices that strengthened her spirit and matured her soul.

She and my children were forced to endure relationships and deal with emotions created by my situation that they would never have "chosen" from a mortal perspective, but they now have a strength that a life of riches and ease could not teach. On the surface, my depression was bad for them, but if it also provided a lesson they asked to learn, then it was also good.

The End of Pain

Please consider the meaning of your life in view of this theodicy —consent and sacrifice.

If you sign a mortgage and agree to pay the bank every month for 30 years, then you don't get the relief from the payments until after 30 years. Trying to stop making payments after 10 years might technically be possible, because nobody can force you not to kill your own mortgage, but reneging on the contract creates a whole other slew of problems for yourself. Even if it seems like the death of the contract will be freeing, you still have to find another place to live, and you lose the chance to own the home without starting over with a new contract for an additional 30 years.

The least problematic way to end a contract is to fulfill the terms early—to accomplish what you agreed to faster than required. The second least problematic relief comes by agreeing to the original terms, for the full term, even if that term is a whole 30 years.

If your suffering, your pain, and your depression, were in fact agreed to in advance—which they had to be for God to be just—then the last resort won't solve the problem, because you will not have accomplished the promises you agreed to. The last resort will only prolong the problem.

The only way to truly make the pain end is to fulfill the agreement as fast as possible. If you agreed to it for *your own* growth or experience, the problem will not go away until you learn and grow to the extent that you agreed. If you agreed to it for someone else, then you made an amazing sacrifice, because that means you agreed that the problem will not go away until *they*—the other parties in your life—learn or gain what *they* needed from your depression agreement! Isn't it obvious now why sometimes you can't make the depression go away or diagnose the problem, no matter how many doctors, or therapists, or "experts" you consult? The theodicy of consent and sacrifice doesn't make the pain end. It only makes the pain meaningful!

If it is even possible to accelerate the process, you would have to ask yourself, "What can I learn from this?" and then actually learn it faster. You would have to ask yourself, "What changes have I been unwilling to try?" and then try them. You would have to ask yourself, "How can I use my pain to help others?" and then actually help, even when it feels like you can't.

This is not fatalism! I never stopped trying to find a physical cure or psychological relief. Sometimes you can pay off the mortgage early, and it's worth trying. But if you can't, the only meaningful relief will come by accepting the pain, not rejecting it.

This theodicy means you have to trust yourself. You have to believe that life is not a random onslaught of pain and suffering, but a deliberate one; that your spiritual, eternal self, the souls of your close friends and family, and the wisdom of your god all chose for your mutual benefit. You have to believe depression is the exact opposite of what it feels—not a punishment, but a blessing.

You know that the opposite doesn't work. Refusing to accept it doesn't make it go away, and doesn't make it easier to deal with. Try it my way. Accept that it was meant to be. Accept that it has meaning. Accept that it has purpose. Accept that it's for the best—even if you don't remember or understand. Yield to the spirit.

Peace

I believe this doctrine primarily for one reason. As I knelt in that prayer, pondering the ramifications of premortal consent, it occurred to me that if I chose my suffering, then those I am hurting chose my suffering too. I don't suffer for nothing. I don't suffer even just for me. I suffer also because they wanted me to do it—for them.

I won't try to prove it with the Bible because this is not a theology book. Yes, I believe scripture supports my assertions, but I believe it foremost because when I articulated that thought, I was overcome with peace. For the first time ever, my suffering had meaning. I believe that peace is God's way of answering prayer and confirming the truth.

I can't go around telling others they asked for it. That would be insane, but it gives me peace to believe that my suffering and their suffering is not in vain!

If you are willing to consider the possibility, despite your doubts, if you are willing to consider that you may have agreed to the pain, if you really want to feel the peace that assures you that everything will be for the best, then I urge you to ask God your own version of this inquiry. "Did I choose this? Is my pain serving a purpose? Did I agree to this?"

I hope God answers your inquiry with peace. If not, ask the question slightly differently, or reword your understanding slightly until He does. As explained in the section on speaking your thoughts, keep talking about it, writing about it, and praying about it, until the words you say truly reflect what you believe and the words "feel right," or at least feel complete.

What is peace? Peace is that sense that no matter how bad it seems, it was meant to be. Peace is the sense that despite the consequences, everything will be okay. Peace is the sense that even if you don't understand the parts, there is meaning in the whole.

For the first time in decades, as I knelt by my bed, my life felt *right*, and not *wrong*. I've ruined my wife's life. I've neglected my children. I've squandered my opportunities. How can this be "right?"

You likely will never know, in this life, the exact meaning of your challenges—only that there is meaning. I cannot tell my wife that in some premortal existence she asked me to be depressed and make her life harder. I cannot prove it. I cannot claim it. Nevertheless, I believe it, because when I articulate that prayer, and *only* that prayer, I feel peace and meaning in my life.

I have said often that I would never have chosen my life experience had I known what I would have to endure. Nevertheless, I believe I did. I chose my life because, on some level, my wife and children needed it, and they asked for it. I chose my life because, on some level, I needed it, and I asked for it.

That is not an excuse. I have no intention of using this belief to pretend any moral superiority or rationalization to sin. Quite the contrary, because I see my challenge from a new perspective, I feel an extra weight of responsibility to endure longer, and to make up for every time my wrongs were *not* beyond my control. I pray that whatever lesson I and they wanted to learn from this experience is done.

I have no excuse to behave with less virtue than I am capable. If I wished this challenge on myself, I did so not because I wanted to give in to it, but because I wanted to fight it. If I chose despair, I must have known I could endure the despair.

This belief does not contradict my Christian faith. I need Jesus for all of those wrongs I have committed with and without intention or control. This belief does not deny Christ—quite the opposite. I give myself to Christ for whatever purpose he chooses, even if his will means I suffer. My faith in Christ allows me to believe all of those inequities, that are beyond my control, can be made right. Whether I am wrong or whether I am right, only Jesus can fix it.

Depression steals from your life. It steals meaning and it steals peace. Whether I agreed to the abyss because I needed it for me or because I sacrificed an easier alternative to help someone else, consent changes everything—consent for me and sacrifice for them, just as they consented to sacrifice for me. I believe this theodicy best explains the truth because it brings meaning to my suffering and restores peace to my soul.

One of the hardest things about life in the bubble of depression is that in that bubble you take more than you give. In the bubble, you don't produce, you only consume. In the bubble, you are too exhausted to give back. In the bubble, you tear others down unintentionally, and constantly. In the bubble, your efforts to work for good or build others up often go misinterpreted and fail.

Whether you actually agreed to your suffering in advance or not, you are exponentially more likely to find peace in your life if you believe it was your choice than if you believe you are a helpless victim! Let me repeat. Whether you agree with me or not, you are more likely to escape the hell when you act as if you chose your circumstances voluntarily!

Even if you find peace with the past, you still need hope that you'll find meaning in your future. Long-lasting purpose and meaning in life requires that you contribute something to the world, and that life has some significance beyond your mere existence. Desperately, at the bottom of the pit, you long to be worth something to someone—anything that will make your life other than a hopeless, purposeless existence. Assume there already is purpose. Assume there already is meaning. Assume you are fulfilling a real responsibility just by the life you agreed to.

Yield to the spirit that designed your life's circumstances from a more enlightened sphere. Your pain is not unfair if you gave your consent. Your pain has purpose if you sacrificed something better for others' benefit.

Part VI: Now what?

19
Responsibility

Let's next talk about how your pain brings additional responsibility—additional meaning. In the eternal scheme of things, you have a responsibility to fulfill whatever you agreed to, but what about here and now? What do you do here and now? What's next? I can think of several possible reactions to this book:

You think it's nonsense

Perhaps you have not experienced severe depression as I have described, or you believe you have overcome depression by your own willpower, or you think this book is nothing but nonsensical, new-age, pseudo-scientific excuses and emotional weakness. Since you have read this book despite my request to the contrary, and you continue to believe that I am misguided, I will not ask you to accept my perception of reality. However, I will beg that you at least consider what I say in the next chapter, "How to Help," about what you can do to help someone like me, who does not see it your way.

You have sympathy

If you have not experienced severe depression and find it difficult to relate to the perspective I shared, but do give me the benefit of the doubt, you have done all I ask. The reason I asked you not to read this book was because I had no expectation that it would help you understand me. When you admit to someone in depression that you don't understand but stand by them anyway, you do help in a real way. That's what you do next. Admit you don't understand. I wrote the next chapter, "How to Help," primarily for you.

Your depression isn't as bad

If you feel "depressed," but did not relate to the extreme metaphors and emotions I shared, I do not dismiss your experience. Your pain is real. What appears like less on the outside may be equal or greater on the inside. I cannot pretend to understand. If you didn't relate to the physical manifestations of depression that I described, then I suspect your depression likely stems more from beliefs rather than biology. If so, you have a responsibility to confront any self-deception. I suspect that you might find more meaningful help in my information on the "12 Lies" that covers the common deceptions and lies in our culture that make coping with life harder than necessary. Please visit MichaelDGriffith.com for more information.

Your depression is worse

If you do relate in some way to my description of hell, but still find no comfort or hope in my perspective, I'm sorry. I don't understand what makes your situation unique. All I can say is that I do understand how it feels when nobody understands. You don't have to try what I say, but please keep trying something.

If you can, find it in you to accept the pain, give up your life to God, and trust whatever crazy justification He might have. I'm not talking religion. I'm talking perspective. Whatever you believe God to be, I suggest you agree now, that if God wants you to suffer, you agree to suffer. Accept that God has a purpose in it even if you do not. Assume that if you choose to submit rather than resent it, then the invisible hand of the divine is obligated to guide your life where it's meant to go. As hard as "yielding to the spirit" may be, even if it's not a divine plan, believing your life has purpose will help you more than believing it does not.

You and I share something

Lastly, you may feel I succeeded at putting into words some of your experience, and see a small glimmer of hope that a new perspective might help. Submit to the challenge with the assumption that you and God designed and agreed to this pain for a reason. Accept that your only reward may be the peace to know that there is meaning, not what that meaning is. Don't pray for the meaning. Pray for the peace. The rest of this chapter might provide a few additional clues to your responsibility.

Productivity

If you cannot yet pursue something more creative and productive with your life, accept that your suffering, in and of itself, has a deliberate although unknown purpose. Believing your pain has purpose for you and others helps. However, real fulfillment in the mortal here and now requires you to produce and offer something to the world.

It's been three years since I first visited the upper cervical chiropractor who changed my life. I tried to work and produce as much as I could while in the pit, but in the pit, everything failed. I quit trying many times, but because I never quit permanently, I eventually found a problem in my neck. Sometimes, a physical change must come before you can produce successfully. I understand that baby steps might be the only steps you can take.

If you already have a great job, produce something of value, and find satisfaction in the service you give to humanity, keep it up. If you don't produce anything for the world, start. If you are not producing something you will not be happy, and you will not be satisfied with the meaning of your life.

While the intangible faith that your life matters in eternity might help, producing real-life tangible results helps more immediately. You have to give something—a job, a skill, a service you sell, a product you make, or financial, moral, or physical support of some kind. Depression sucks you into a self-centered bubble against your will, and you can never fully escape it unless you interact with others and provide something of value. You have to have a responsibility and produce something that improves others' lives.

Complaining about the injustice of the world will never get you out of the pit. Working to produce something that eases that injustice will. Are you productive? I propose a simple two-part test.

1. **Are you producing or consuming?**
   Some complaints, political activism, and fault-finding can inspire others to change the world. However, most of the time, such actions are more destructive than productive. Even if you inspire change, those you inspire do the actual producing, not you. You must produce something of value to not be depressed. Tearing down a broken system is not productive unless you are building an alternative. Stopping others from producing is not productive. Ask yourself, are you consuming or producing?

2. **If others knew everything about your motivations and your capability, would they pay for what you produce?**
   I know monetary compensation is an imperfect measure of value, but the principle is sound. People generally only pay for a win-win arrangement. If others are willing to pay, they believe you are producing something of value.

What do you have to give? What can you produce?

You Understand

I've said it so many times already that it has become cliché, but those who haven't experienced real depression don't understand real depression. They don't understand—but you do!

Those who have been depressed for a day don't know what it's like to be depressed for a week, and those who have been depressed for a week don't know what it's like to be flattened for a month. Those who have been devastated for a month don't understand being imprisoned for a year, or dead to the world for decades.

Wherever you fall on that spectrum, you know something "they" don't know. I can't call it a silver lining. I would rather not know. I wish I didn't understand. I wish I could go back to the naivety I knew before depression, when I felt in control and I could judge others freely in ignorant bliss. But I can't. I can't go back. I can't unknow what I know now.

You can't unknow what you know. Unfortunately, that means that you have a responsibility that those who have never been in that pit cannot fulfill. Only you can understand how it feels when "they" don't understand, and so the responsibility falls on you to be one of the "us."

You can choose to stay silent and keep your pain personal, and if you do, I understand. However, because only you understand, you have something that only you can give. "They" cannot give what they do not understand. You can. That alone can be meaningful, even if you don't know any other skill or service you can give to the world in your present circumstances.

Personally, I feel like the depression stole everything from me. Even though I have emerged partly from that pit, my brain no longer works the way it used to. I used to do computer programming and teach financial planning, but my brain just can't concentrate on numbers the way it used to. Because of depression, I've fallen at least 15 years behind in my professional knowledge, and any new career would require starting from scratch.

Honestly, that is the main reason why I write this book. I don't want to share all of this personal stuff. It's just that I know that I need to produce something, give something to the world, and the lessons of depression are the only thing I have left right now. The depression stole everything else. Since I do have a perspective on depression that I hope can benefit someone, I produce this book for the simple reason that I don't know what else I have to give.

I know you did not choose the torment either, at least not in this life, but you have it now. You understand something they don't understand, and that gives you a responsibility to use your understanding for good.

You Don't Understand

Depression, by itself, gives you responsibility. If nothing else, depression should change the way you see life—change the way you see "them."

They don't understand. Worse, they don't understand that they don't understand. I have written tens of thousands of words, trying to prove an exception, that maybe I do understand a little bit of what you feel. Yet, you probably still feel that you suffer in a unique way that no one, including me, can understand.

Please take solace in the best consolation I can offer. You may not truly understand my experience, and I may not truly understand yours, but we both understand what it's like to have nobody else understand. We both know what it's like to be alone, and we are not alone in that.

What's my point?

If you have experienced the irresolvable certainty of that loneliness, then not only do you understand that they don't understand you, you also understand that you don't understand them.

You don't understand physical abuse, or rape, or slavery. You don't understand cancer, or diabetes, cerebral palsy, Alzheimer's, Parkinson's, anorexia, autism, migraines, ADD, MS, MD, ED, BPH, CFS, or IBS. You don't understand what it's like to raise a child with physical, mental, or social disabilities. You don't understand the challenges of poverty, discrimination, atypical sexual identity, addiction, torture, or war. You don't understand parenthood, divorce, old age, death, natural disaster. You don't really understand any of it—unless you have experienced it yourself.

Depression changed the way I view the world. It changed how I view "them." I used to have all the answers, and knew what they needed to hear. Now, not only do I know that they don't understand me, I also know that I don't understand them. I feel confident saying that if your unique experience doesn't give you less judgment, more compassion, and more patience with them, then you need more of it to learn that lesson.

I completely understand that in the chains of that pit your demon hurls out insults and judgment with no patience and no selfless concern. It feels like hell because your demon forces inappropriate emotions on you. It feels so very wrong because deep down inside you know that you have no more right to feel so much disgust and irritation with them than they have to judge you.

If you had already given into that demon, if you had already given into the disgust and hatred, you wouldn't still be listening to me. The fact that you continue reading tells me that in your soul you recognize the contradiction. The fact that you are still listening tells me that you understand that you don't understand them any better than they understand you. If that is true, then you are not losing the battle. You are winning.

Depression makes you feel guilty because you've done so many things to cause hurt, but if you recognize the hurt and renounce the hurt, you are not losing. You are winning.

Depression is one gigantic contradiction. Depression might make you feel the hatred, but you hate the hatred. If the depression has taught you to long for compassion and seek an escape from the selfishness, you are not losing. You are winning!

In the depths of hell, you will gravitate toward one of two extremes. Sometimes you just want to pull everyone else down in the pit with you. *Life is not fair. It would only be fair if they suffered too.* On the other hand, sometimes we consider the alternative. Sometimes, because you know what the pit is like, you want nothing more than to help others stay out of it. You feel both inclinations. As long as you still feel both and strive for the latter, you are not losing. You are winning!

Because you have been in the pit you have a responsibility and understanding unlike any other. You can give a gift that others cannot or will not give. You can give something that you desperately wish others would have given you.

What can you give?

Other people live in that pit! You can be the only person that understands that "they" don't understand. You can be the only person that understands that *you* don't understand. Because of undiagnosed physical problems and unrecognized cultural deceptions, you may not be able to pull others out of the pit, but maybe, just maybe, because of you, they won't be alone.

To find "meaning" you have to give something to the world. "They" don't understand, and to everyone else in the pit, the "they" is you. If nothing else, let it be your responsibility to acknowledge to others in the pit that you understand that you don't understand.

THE END

NOTE: The preceding text was written only for those who have experienced severe depression. If you have not, the descriptions may not have made sense—or like hours of wasted excuses, rationalization, and justifications for bad behavior. On the contrary, this final chapter is a separate text written for those who have not been severely depressed themselves but wish to help someone they don't understand, who is caught in depression's grasp.

20
How to Help

You know how in late summer, when you are just trying to relax and minding your own business—then a fly lands on your nose? Somehow, it finds you and it won't go away. It tickles your nose, and when you shoo it away, you think it's gone, but it's not. Like a rubber ball on a string it keeps coming back. On your cheek … on your arm … in your hair.

You try to ignore it, but you can't. You can barely detect its tiny little legs, but your attention keeps getting diverted anyway. Those minuscule vibrations on your body hair and skin compound on each other until you can think of nothing else. You shoo. You swat. You flail. You readjust your body position or dart into another room to avoid that fly. Nevertheless, it seems once that fly finds you it won't leave you alone. That rubber ball on the string keeps snapping back at you. You start to feel phantom tickling all over your body. You start to sense that fly, even when it's not there. It's on your arm … no, your ear … your shoe …*Is it on my face again? … Are there two flies now?*

That fly carries disease. Flies are the adult form of maggots that grow into life feeding on rotting excrement. Now, they are dancing on your lips. You shudder at the thought. Flick them off. Wash your hands. Wash your face. Cover your face. Turn off the lights. But the fly returns—again and again.

Depression, like that fly, is an irritant that keeps bouncing back in your face.

On a good day—when I'm not wallowing in the pit—I get annoyed, I stand up, I grab a fly swatter, and the fly dies! End of story.

On a bad day, the fly is more than a literal fly. The fly represents every demon in life that is impossible to kill. On a bad day, when I'm "depressed," the fly triggers a cascade of negativity.

> *That @*#$% fly!*
> *I hate that @*#$% fly!*
> *I hate my @*#$% life!*
>
> *It's not fair! I can't even relax or try to work without a fly, or another problem.*
>
> *This always happens! As soon as I try anything, a $#%* fly comes and makes me sick!*
>
> *Why me?! ... Why do the flies love me?! ... What's wrong with me?!*
>
> *I might as well just give up.*
>
> *I know I'll miss. If I try to kill it, I'll miss. I'm bad at killing flies! I'm bad at everything!*
>
> *Knowing me ... I will kill it, and then I'll wash up and another one will come anyway. Or I will kill it, and it will be one of those juicy ones that splatters all over ... And then I'll have another mess to clean up ... And then I won't have time to do anything better.*
>
> *Whatever happens, I know it will make me sick. It will stress me out, and I'll pull a muscle, or I'll trip and fall. I always screw it up somehow! I'll waste even more time! I'll do something stupid that will cost money I don't have!*
>
> *I don't have enough energy to fail again. I'm better off not trying ... I just have to live with it ... It sucks, but not*

trying is better than failing. I can't handle another failure. I'm too weak.

What difference will it make anyway? It's not helping anybody but me! It's always about me! ... I'm so selfish! ... I have to suffer! I have no other choice! I either suffer with the fly, or if I try to kill it, I suffer worse!

Life is hell! I hate my #*%@$* life! ...

I deserve it. I'm so worthless! ... What's the point? If by some miracle I kill it, there will just be another fly anyway!

I'm already mad, and now my bad attitude will drag everyone else down. My relationships are going to get even worse now! It's too late! ... I can't hide my irritation now, and everyone will take offense no matter what I say. I'll hurt everyone and ruin their day. I've already ruined their lives anyway!

It would be better for everyone if I just weren't here at all!

I know it doesn't seem rational. No writer would use that many exclamation points in real life, but in depression, every thought feels intense. Every speculation down the cascade into hell carries an intense emotional charge—and ironically, when every thought is emphasized, no thought is emphasized. When every thought screams, you can't even really hear any of them, and perhaps more importantly, you can't hear anything else either.

This explanation is 100% literal. In the pit of depression, I feel exactly this way about actual, literal flies. This explanation is also 100% metaphorical. In the pit of depression, every injustice, imperfection, and inadequacy in life feels like another fly.

When I'm not depressed, I can deal with life's flies—life's problems. I attack the challenges and try to make life better. I kill the flies.

When I'm depressed, I can't kill the fly. I don't mean I refuse to kill the fly. I don't mean I don't want to kill the fly. I mean, I *can't* kill the fly. The very act of trying to kill the fly generates an emotional vortex of negativity that sucks every life challenge in and stacks them on top of each other. The very act of trying to think positively and optimistically about killing a real fly only highlights the negative emotions in contrast. The problems mount. Before long, I can think of nothing else—nothing but all the metaphorical flies in life and their annoying, disgusting, disease ridden attraction to me. I become paralyzed, unable to do anything else until the fly dies—but I can't kill the fly myself. I know everyone else can kill flies easily. I can't!

If you have not personally suffered severe depression, it seems so trivial to just kill the fly and be done with it. That's what you don't understand. We really can't just kill the fly. You can, yes. It seems like we should be able to do the same.

From where you stand it looks like I won't do something so easy to help myself—I *won't* kill the fly. From where I stand, I *can't* kill the fly. No amount of explanation will convince you why we *can't* do something that you find so easy. I'm not asking you to understand something you can't understand. I'm asking you to understand that you don't understand—that we really do see and feel it differently.

In the middle of depression's assault on my brain, my brain literally cannot think the way your brain thinks. No matter how much it seems like I should be able to take that simple step and kill the fly, no matter how obvious or rational you and others find it, no matter how emotional, lazy, or overreacting I appear, you can't help me when you assume the problem feels the same way to me that it feels to you.

To you, the fly is the problem.

To me, the fly is not the problem! The fly is the final straw on a heap of bigger crises that will break the camel's back if I even try to address it.

The litany of crises I'm trying to juggle is much more weighty and complicated than I can articulate in the moment, and so it appears I cannot even handle a measly fly. It's not the fly. The fly triggers an emotional maelstrom that draws my ruminations to the weight of everything else that I have been trying to ignore. The emotional leviathan whose back that fly rides dumps it all on me at once.

The weight of that fly is one milligram too much. We have much bigger problems than the fly. Our careers, our relationships, our finances, our health, and our faith are all screwed up. We don't know how to fix them. We've tried and failed, and been left hopeless. If I try to kill that fly and fail again—if I can't even do something as simple as swat a fly—I risk pushing my emotional triggers past the point of no return. I'd rather suffer in a selfish bubble of fly tickling annoyance, believing that killing the fly is still possible, than fail at the most menial of tasks and remove the last faint flicker of hope that I have any control at all.

I realize you have those life problems too. The difference is your brain manages it differently. Something in my body, or hormones, or brain is broken!

It's not about the fly.

It's about me.

My problem is not the fly.

My problem is me.

Killing the fly won't fix me!

> *I am broken and worthless ... so why even try to kill the fly?*

That's stupid. That's illogical. That makes no sense.

True. My logic is completely preposterous, but it's also completely real. The worst thing you can do is try to explain to me how stupid it is, and how irrational it is, and how imaginary it is. It's not imaginary! The feelings are imaginary to you, and when you fail to understand that my perception differs from yours, you are not actually helping. You are making the problem worse.

To a depressed person, their own logic, no matter how flawed on the outside, is very real on the inside. Their logic must work around a whirlwind of emotions that you cannot see. They cannot

How to Help

adequately express those emotions to you when you haven't felt them, don't understand them, or belittle them. Nevertheless, their fears are justified. If you could understand the emotions, which attack them involuntary, you would see how their logic makes sense. Their actions or inactions are based on real life experience. They are protecting themselves from the environment. They are protecting themselves from others. They are protecting themselves from themselves. Yes, there are real factors on the outside that their misguided reasoning doesn't properly take into account, but there are also real factors on the inside that your well-intentioned reasoning can't take into account. If you admit your internal computer reacts differently, you can't assume you know how their emotions and logic will work.

They are not choosing between a good solution and a bad solution. They are choosing between two bad solutions. Killing the fly is not necessarily the right solution for them just because it's the most obvious solution to you. Sometimes, the obvious thing really will make it worse for them. That is partly why depression is hell. Killing the fly might actually make their internal emotions worse. Sometimes, all available options bring you closer to a nuclear meltdown. From the inside of depression there is often no right answer. They are not choosing between killing the fly and living with the fly. They are not choosing between eliminating the problem and living with the problem. The depressed mind is choosing between the emotional cocoon of living with the torment of the fly, or risking an emotional catastrophe by trying to kill the fly. No matter what it looks like from the outside, sometimes they really can't kill the fly for themselves.

How can you help?

Give the Benefit of the Doubt

Stop blaming me for what you don't understand and start giving me the benefit of the doubt.

If I'm just lazy and making excuses, maybe I do need a good kick in the pants. On the other hand, if it's actually "depression," then I'm not actually capable of what you are asking. Knocking me down when I'm already in a hole won't help.

If your actions prove to me that you don't understand my reality, I won't trust you. When I don't trust you, it doesn't matter if you are right or wrong; I won't listen. I don't have the energy to sort out good advice from patronizing judgment, and I will discount whatever you say.

I'm asking you to give me the benefit of the doubt.

Best-case scenario—I which is probably the truth—I am doing the best I can, even if you can't see it. By giving me the benefit of the doubt you won't solve the problem, but you will stop becoming part of the problem.

Worst-case scenario—I really am a loser who isn't even trying. However, even if I really do need an attitude adjustment to climb out of the pit, I'm not going to climb toward someone who is condescending or pushing me down, I'm going to climb toward someone who believes me.

If you want to help, you have to follow one simple rule—give me the benefit of the doubt.

Guilt tripping me won't work. I already feel guilty.

If I seem rude, assume it's not malicious.

If I refuse help, assume I have a good reason.

If I contradict you, don't argue.

Giving the benefit of the doubt is very simple, but it's not easy. It's very hard. Admit you don't understand me, and despite all the evidence to the contrary, trust that I act with good intentions.

If you can't give me the benefit of the doubt, leave me alone. I do not have the energy or ability to make you understand. If you won't believe me, you become part of the problem. You become an irritating fly on a string that I don't know how to deal with. If you can't give me the benefit of the doubt, cut that string and leave me alone.

Giving the benefit of the doubt means accepting that it might take a really long time for me to change on my own. You might have to endure my emotional roller coaster for years. It's not fair to you at all. I really am sorry, but unless you can give me the benefit of the doubt, it will take even longer.

If you *can* give me the benefit of the doubt, keep reading through the following suggestions that provide more specifics.

Admit You Don't Understand

Stop expecting an explanation. Why am I mad? Why did I leave? Why am I crying? What was I thinking? What did I mean by that? Sometimes I don't know. Sometimes I do know, but I can't explain it to you. Sometimes I do know, but I want to spare your feelings. Sometimes I do know, but I want to avoid your reaction that I know will make me feel worse. Stop expecting an explanation. You can ask for an explanation, but giving me the benefit of the doubt also means accepting no answer as a sufficient answer.

Giving you an explanation is like trying to explain the taste of salt to someone who doesn't already know, trying to explain color to a blind man, or trying to explain sex to a toddler. The explanation sounds weird. The explanation might be *accepted*, but it can never be truly understood if you have not experienced it.

Think of your greatest accomplishment. Can anyone else on Earth really understand what you went through? Think of your greatest failure. Can anyone else on Earth really understand the personal nuances of your circumstances? Does anyone else really understand?

Telling me that you know how I feel won't help. Telling me about your own or others' suffering is not true understanding! You can only empathize with the depressed version of me if you also share the experience of not being understood. Don't empathize with the depression. Empathize with the loneliness.

I believe I can say categorically that if you can't admit that you don't understand me, then you have never been "depressed" like me. Thinking that you do understand or trying to prove that you can relate, only reinforces to me that you don't. The more you know what's best for me, the more you prove to me that you don't understand me at all.

If you truly know what it means to not be understood—to be truly alone—you would never assume that you understand. I'm just asking you to admit it. You cannot help if I don't trust you, and I cannot trust you if you don't admit it. Let's all say it together, what should be the universal common experience of humanity: "I'm sorry, I don't understand."

Believe Me

Giving me the benefit of the doubt means believing me. I know you say you believe in me. Even if that's true, I don't just need you to believe *IN* me; I need you to actually believe me.

If I tell you I can't kill the fly, believe me.

If I say I'm about to lose it, assume I'm not exaggerating.

If I say I won't, don't expect me to try.

If I ask you not to do something, don't do it.

If I say I hate something, don't contradict me.

In romantic comedy cliché dialogue, "Don't tell me how to feel." Feel free to disagree, but that doesn't change that I really do believe what I say.

Whatever I say, no matter how bizarre, believe me. You know those irrational things I say when I express strange desires and doubts? I'm trying to explain confusing things that cannot be explained. I'm trying to open up to a friend, and when you dismiss them, contradict them, or don't believe them, you make it impossible to ask you for help.

Just the other day, I was teetering on the verge of tears. The gaping chasm of emotional freefall was about to open underneath me, and I knew it. I held my external facade together as best I could for as long as I could, and in that least opportune moment, my wife needed "to talk." I told my wife I didn't feel well, and couldn't talk. I told the truth. I did the right thing by trying to prevent the blowout that would happen if I didn't stop the conversation. Of course, because I had already started slipping into the downward spiral of depression, the words didn't come out in the most kind way. Nevertheless, it was the kindest explanation I could muster in my emotional state.

When I say "I can't talk right now," believe me. Don't read into it. I'm not saying "I don't want to talk." When I say "I can't talk right now," I really mean "I *can't* talk right now." When you force the conversation anyway, I will blow up or blow out. It all could be prevented if you actually believed me.

That is why I don't tell my wife the truth. If I don't say anything, I get blamed for not saying anything. If I try to explain how I feel and it comes out wrong, I get blamed for how it comes out. Worse, because she doesn't really understand, if she doesn't believe what I say, she trusts me less, and I trust her less too. She still feels bad, but I feel worse too. I lose either way—and so does she. If the truth causes more pain than the silence, I will choose silence.

You don't have to agree with what I say. I'm not asking you to validate anything that's untrue. You only have to believe me. You have to believe that I sincerely believe what I say. I ask you to believe me, even though I lie to you all the time. I don't want to lie to you, but I feel like I have to lie, because you don't believe me when I don't. It's easier for you to believe what you want to believe, than to believe what I tell you. You can't help me if you don't accept the truth, and I will never tell you the truth if I can't trust you. If you start believing me, maybe I'll start telling you the truth.

Stop Trying to Fix It

Maybe the problem really is all in my head. So what. You can't impose a solution if it's in my head. You can change the external environment, but you can't fix what's in my head. Stop trying! Giving me the benefit of the doubt means *not* assuming you have the answer.

People who love you find it difficult to admit that they can't help. I've tried over and over to explain to my wife that she can't help. She doesn't believe me.

Please understand—you can't help. You can't fix the problem. No matter what you think will help, you are wrong, because even the right thing on paper won't work if I don't accept it. You can't help, because "helpfulness" doesn't depend on you willfully offering the "right" thing. Actual "help" depends on my willfully receiving and accepting the "right" thing.

When my back—and brain—begin to crack under the stress, you might sympathetically, sincerely, lovingly want to remove the straws off the metaphorical camel's back. Don't! The very act of inserting yourself into my life, making assumptions about what I need, and encouraging me to follow your suggestions—even if you have good intentions—may make you the final straw that breaks the camel's back. Even if your help should be appreciated in a rational world, by forcing it on me without my ability to prepare for it, you necessarily add weight to my back before any chance at relief.

Even if you are "right," you cannot dictate the terms of the "help." Offering me a ladder out of the pit won't help if I can't climb it. I can't get out of the pit without help, and you can't help without my ability to climb. Accept the one thing you don't want to believe; you can't help—at least not on your own terms.

Don't impose your time or money or advice. You can offer help, but give me the benefit of the doubt if I refuse.

Ask, or Let Me Ask

Giving me the benefit of the doubt means trusting what I say I need over what you think I need. Don't give me what I "need," give me what I ask. Yes, it seems very inefficient. It is. You might be right about what I need, but it will only help if I ask for it.

Years ago, in the middle of my years-long abyss, our dishwasher broke. I, or my wife, or kids, must have mentioned it at church or on social media, or somewhere in passing. Who knows? All I know is that a surprise gift of a new dishwasher showed up at my front porch.

It seemed obvious. Our dishwasher broke and we "needed" a new dishwasher. From the outside, it seemed like a great service to us since we had no income at the time. Some well-meaning person wanted to help—but they didn't ask! I didn't ask for a dishwasher, and they didn't ask if I wanted a dishwasher.

They probably felt great about giving me something I "needed." I understand if they thought buying the dishwasher was better than handing out cash. I understand that the giver probably thought a low-end dishwasher was better than no dishwasher. I get that they were trying to create the feeling of joy and surprise, but a depressed person doesn't need the stress of joy and surprise. A depressed person "needs" only what they are prepared to *receive*, not what you are prepared to *give*.

That dishwasher surprise sent me spiraling into the pit. I could not handle the stress of a new dishwasher that I didn't ask for. My routine had already incorporated hand washing the dishes, and I had much bigger financial problems and much more pressing financial needs at the time. The broken dishwasher was not even close to my biggest stress. If they really wanted to help, my kids needed clothes more than they needed self-cleaning dishes. The dishwasher gift only proved to me that the anonymous giver didn't actually know anything about my real problems. I felt like they wasted hundreds of dollars on a gift, when if they had just asked, something else would have helped more. It felt like they cared more about giving a gift to feel good about themselves, than actually helping me. The gift forced me to focus on the installation, and changing the routine, and trying to have a good attitude about an appliance that I would never choose for myself, instead of focusing on my real problems. I resented the gift, because it felt uncaring and refocused my attention on other triggers.

Because it was a low end dishwasher, it broke very quickly, and we couldn't even get it repaired. The gift of a dishwasher was actually the gift of stress—stress of resentment, stress of the installation, stress of misguided priorities, stress of the breakdown, and still no working dishwasher. More stress is the last thing you should give a depressed person. I blamed the anonymous giver for making my life harder. When depressed, I feel loathing whether it makes sense or not. I can be grateful for their helpful intentions, and still more miserable and resentful because of it. If they had asked, I would have preferred any amount of cash, no matter how small, over which I could maintain control. Depression makes you feel out of control, and having no control over the dishwasher only made the depression worse.

I realize my wife and kids actually appreciated the dishwasher, while it worked. That's not a good reason not to ask me first. Just because their concerns are valid doesn't mean mine are not. If I had been asked, I would have at least had the opportunity to discuss it with my wife first, and felt at least some control.

I'm not saying don't give gifts. Other depressed people might not resent the gift the same as I did. My point is that you can't assume you are helping unless you ask, or I ask. Don't ask me "How are you?" or I might say, "Not good, my dishwasher broke," and you might assume I want a new dishwasher.

Rather, ask me "What can I do to help?" I might not let you help if you ask. I might say nothing. But eventually, if you trust me enough to allow me to make my own decisions—if you give me the benefit of the doubt—I will tell you what to do.

Depending on the person, it may be more hugs, or less. It may be more encouragement and more service, or less. It may be more social time and activity, or less. It may be more money and more gifts, or less. It may be conversation, or distraction, or silence—or nothing.

You'll never know unless I tell you—and you believe the answer. Don't assume. Ask me, or let me ask you.

Mirroring

Giving the benefit of the doubt means validating my depression rather than trying to change it. One simple rule of human relations applies to almost every emotion. People want to share their feelings. If the cheesecake tastes amazing, I want those that I love to experience the same ecstasy. When we eat, or dance, or make love, we want to share the feeling with others. When others whisper, I whisper. When they yawn, I yawn. When I laugh, I don't want to laugh alone. I want everyone to laugh—and the more everyone laughs, the more I enjoy the humor.

However, it works both ways. When someone hurts you, you secretly wish they would be hurt—even if you don't reciprocate publicly. When someone yells at you in anger, you want to yell too. At least you feel the anger too, even if you don't show it. Likewise, when you feel depressed, you want others to feel depressed.

Miserable people want others to share their misery. "Misery loves company," as they say. Wanting others to share your misery makes depression even harder. Rationally, you want others to be happy and live their best lives, but when you feel miserable, you can't help but want other to share the misery. At best, you at least want others to understand the misery so that you are not alone.

You wouldn't brag about dancing, to a friend whose recent accident confined her to a wheelchair. You wouldn't even hint that a paraplegic should try to stand. You wouldn't flaunt your money in front of a child in poverty. You wouldn't gloat about the cheesecake in front of someone on a feeding tube. That would be cruel.

Yet for some reason, when I am depressed, you try to cheer me up. You try to make me happy. You try to be fun. You try to make me laugh. You try to be optimistic. You show off the very thing I can't have and expect it to make me feel better. I no longer have positive thoughts to stand on, and you are trying to force me to stand.

You are assuming I can stand on a positive attitude just by changing my mind. You are assuming I can stand on a broken leg. I can't. I might play along and pretend—but really, all you are doing is proving to me that you don't understand. When I am exhausted, hopeless, and crying, I don't need you to be full of energy, smiles, and optimism. I need you to cry.

I can't count the number of times I have had to leave a room because the people in that room were too happy. It is less miserable to dwell with the damned souls in hell than to share heaven with the angels when you cannot also share the angels' joy.

Meet me where I am, not where you want me to be. It is called mirroring. You talk the speed I talk. If I am monotone, you are monotone. If I lack energy, you should lack energy.

If you listened to this book's script as an audiobook, you might have found it dull and monotone. Typically, authors hire voice actors who can dramatize their writing and make the audio more engaging. I'm intentionally avoiding excess drama, because people in the middle of depression don't feel that way. They don't want me to pretend to be happy. If I tried to read this script with more expression, it might sound better to you, but to someone who was depressed it would sound fake. When you can't feel the joy, it's hard to believe that those who do aren't faking it.

> *Real joy would be an act for me, so how can it be real for you?*

Yes, you can cheer me up. You can try to get me to laugh, and you can be optimistic, but not if you don't meet me where I am first. You can't take me from zero to ten. You first have to take me from zero to one.

Mirror my perception, not yours.

Kill Flies

You cannot do anything to change my insides. You can, however, change the environment outside.

You can kill flies!

You might not understand why it's so hard for me to kill the fly myself. You might not understand why I won't get a job, go to church, hang out with friends, visit your mother, clean the house, or give you the attention you deserve and ask for. You might not understand why I say I can't or won't do something—or even try. You might resent doing for me what I should do for myself.

Nevertheless, giving me the benefit of the doubt means doing for me what I won't or can't do for myself. If the fly weighs me down, irritates me, or creates an overreaction in me—kill the fly for me, please! As long as I ask, or you ask and I agree, kill the fly!

When I hit rock bottom, my wife had to get more schooling and get a new career to provide the support for our family that I failed to provide. She didn't do it out of some charitable mercy on me. She did it out of necessity, and probably with plenty of resentment toward me. She started supporting me financially. She had to abandon life as she knew it. She had to give up time with the children. She had to accept a certain amount of chaos in parts of her life. She had to sacrifice a lot of physical and emotional pleasure—all because I wouldn't do it.

On top of all my other problems, the need to provide financial support for the family was such an enormous weight on my back that I could not even lift a finger to kill a fly for myself. Neither of us really understood that, but by removing such an immense burden from me, it actually allowed my mind to be freed just enough that I could start climbing out of the pit.

You cannot pull me out of a pit that is all in my head, but you can remove irritations and burdens on the outside that will make it easier for me to climb for myself. If you can do something huge like take care of my job, or finances, or children, physical health, or security—and I agree—then that huge relief of burden helps more than any psychological coping mechanism.

On the other hand, if you have no way to do more than kill a literal fly that irritates me, kill the fly. That fly—that irritation, that trigger—stops me from seeing reality as you see it. That fly forces me to concentrate on my selfish little bubble of pain, and until that fly dies I won't even be able to see the ladder out of the pit, even if you're telling me all about it. If that's all you can do, please kill the fly.

Remove the weight from my shoulder a little bit here and a little bit there, until I can breathe well enough that I'm no longer drowning. Take a little more responsibility on yourself to lessen the burden on me.

No, it's not fair! I'm seemingly asking you to enable my bad behavior. You deserve the respect, not me. I should give the sacrifice to you, not the other way around. I'm asking you to give me the benefit of the doubt when I don't deserve it, even when I am in the wrong.

All of that is true. I know I'm asking the impossible. If you would rather just walk away and leave me alone, I totally understand. I'm not telling you what I deserve. I'm telling you what I need. If you want to help, I'm telling you how. Every metaphorical and literal fly you assassinate for me, no matter how small, takes weight off my shoulders and helps me not dwell on the hopelessness.

As long as I ask, or you ask and I agree, kill flies.

Only one person in my life followed these rules—my father. I suspect that those who know him would never suspect he was actually my biggest help. As I climbed ever so gradually out of depression's pit, he had a fall in his old age from which he would never recover. He lived just long enough, and with enough mental clarity, for everyone to have time with him and say goodbye. I only wanted to tell him one thing.

Over the years, he knew something was wrong with my health, but he didn't understand. He knew I asked for help more than he thought I should, and he didn't understand. He knew I changed my faith, refused work, and declined opportunities that he would have accepted. Nevertheless, he didn't try to fix me. Honestly, knowing him, even I was shocked at how little he judged me for acting in ways he didn't understand. Instead, he believed me, and killed flies for me when I asked for help. He was the only person who acted that way. Before he passed, I only had one thing to say. "Dad, thank you for always giving me the benefit of the doubt." He appreciated that I noticed, and acknowledged that he did, in fact, not understand my perspective. He confessed that he did, in fact, give me the benefit of the doubt—on purpose.

I ask you to do the same for anyone you know who suffers in depression's grasp.

For whatever it's worth, thank you.

Afterword

Physical cause or not, all depression is made worse by holding onto some untruths. Emotions beyond our control make it easy to believe the lies that the devil, with his religious and political allies, would use to manipulate us.

Professionally, I have spent decades studying the psychology of persuasion. My professional experience with persuasion combined with my personal experience in the pit of depression has given me a surprising clarity about the deceptions that pervade our society. If you believe learning to identify those lies might be useful to you, please visit my website, MichaelDGriffith.com, for more information on the "12 lies" that make your life harder.

Suggestions?

If you have suffered from severe depression and would like to add suggestions: 1) describing how depression feels to you; 2) sharing how you have coped; or 3) suggesting how you like others to help, please write to feedback@TheyDontUnderstand.com. I will update this manuscript with ideas that I find appropriate.

Help the Cause

I understand that in the pit of depression, you very likely do not have extra money to seek help and support. Because I don't want anyone with depression to suffer alone when I can prevent it, I make an e-book or audiobook available to anyone who requests it, free of charge. Please visit TheyDontUnderstand.com.

If you received this book free of charge and *do* have the means to support me in this effort, please buy the e-book for whatever amount you can afford at TheyDontUnderstand.com

Appendix: Summary

Below, I summarize the principles and steps that we discussed, which may help you find some measure of relief and some measure of meaning in your life.

The Rules

1. Promise that death will be the last resort, only after you try the things you don't want to try.
2. Promise to endure at least ____ (fill in the blank) more years.
3. Promise to do what is best for others, not just for yourself.
4. Promise to never take your life at the lowest point.
5. Commit to the truth.
6. Take one step at a time.

Possible Baby Steps

Strengthen the Body

- Use traditional medicine to relieve any physical ailment, even if seemingly unrelated to depression.
- Consider antidepressant drugs.

- Try changing the quantity, frequency, schedule, or composition of your diet.
- Eliminate food and environmental stress to test for toxicities.
- Supplement to alleviate potential deficiencies.
- Try changing the method, intensity, or schedule of how you move and exercise.
- Get quality rest when asleep and find respite when awake.
- Try alternative medicine.

Govern the Mind

- Find cooperative, non-competitive relationships.
- Give your sins to God even if you don't believe. Forgive yourself, even if others don't—even if you don't deserve it.
- Quit pretending and give true explanations to those who may be able to help.
- Ask for specific help, even if "they" judge you or say no.
- Decide to be responsible for your own reactions.
- Take proactive steps to avoid potential triggers. Repeat often enough to form new habits.
- Recognize lies that you believe, which make your life harder.
- Consider working with a qualified, cooperative therapist.

Yield to the Spirit

- Act as if you designed your life's challenges intentionally, or at a minimum consented to them.
- Assume that God will use your pain and the unintentional harm you cause to work for others' good.
- Ask what you should learn from your trials, and assume a responsibility to use that knowledge for others' benefit.
- Don't pray for answers; pray for peace.
- Adopt a responsibility to produce something that makes the world better.
- Admit to others that you don't understand.

Acknowledgements

Without some very specific help over the last few decades, I do not believe I could even be alive, let alone able to write this book. Thank you to my family, who endured years of my failures as I started to get sicker. Thank you to all those who provided very significant medical, financial, and material aid to my family when I failed to provide. Thank you to my wife, Kristy, who in her own dark struggle made huge sacrifices to become the family breadwinner. She literally saved my life.

In retrospect, having accepted that my hellhole was meant to be, thank you to my God for allowing me to participate in something this meaningful—even though I don't understand, and even though I struggle for that gratitude to be sincere.

Especial thanks to Dr. Jeffrey Forest, who made it possible to receive chiropractic care I needed, but could not arrange on my own. Thank you to several unnamed families who have lost children and loved ones to suicide, that inspired me to share my inner thoughts. Thank you to the amazingly creative Cydney Neil, who trusted me, and who provided truly insightful perspectives of faith, depression, and business.

Thank you to everyone and anyone who, at times, and especially my father, who always gave me the benefit of the doubt.

www.ingramcontent.com/pod-product-compliance
Lightning Source LLC
Chambersburg PA
CBHW070100080526
44586CB00013B/1134